# THE BOOT ROOM BOYS

To Geraldine, Tom and Ella

# THE BOOT ROOM BOYS

## The Unseen Story of Anfield's Conquering Heroes

Virgin BOOKS

# Content

# Introduction

Legend has it that if ever the symbolic Liver Birds fly away from their perch on top of the magnificent Royal Liver Building on Liverpool's historic waterfront, the city will cease to exist. For many years Everton supporters used to mock Liverpool fans by claiming the Liver Birds would fly away before Liverpool won the FA Cup. Liverpool had been beaten FA Cup finalists in 1914 and 1950, and the club and fans were desperate to win the coveted trophy and emulate Everton's successes of 1906 and 1933. In those days before the arrival of Bill Shankly, Everton were actually regarded as the bigger club in the city, but things were soon to change. In many ways the story of the 'Boot Room Boys' is the 'before and after' tale of Bill Shankly and his loyal back room staff. If the post-war years and the 1950s were in monochrome, then the 1960s burst into colour. Bill Shankly even changed the kit from red shirts, white shorts and red and white socks to the distinctive all-red kit everyone knows today.

Liverpool in the 1960s would not only become the centre of world attention because of The Beatles and Merseybeat; also, remarkably,

*Liverpool FC, 1965.*

from the embarrassment of a Second Division nightmare, Shankly would revolutionise the club and turn a sleeping giant into a European force. He was able to do this by harnessing the collective endeavour and the natural enthusiasm of his trusted lieutenants. When he arrived at Anfield, he crucially decided to keep on the back room staff who were already there. He asked for loyalty and honesty and, during his reign, he certainly got those values in abundance.

Post-war Liverpool was a vibrant, bustling city of 765,000 souls, with the River Mersey and the docks its beating heart. Numerous factories employed tens of thousands of people, and for many of these people, football at the weekend was their religion. Liverpool had suffered tremendously during the dark days of the Second World War. As the second port of the Empire, it imported a third of the UK's food and goods, so became a target for Hitler's Luftwaffe. It was an attempt to disrupt trade and communications during the longest battle of the Second World War, the Battle of the Atlantic.

Rationing and hardship continued well after the war, and football was a welcome escape from the dreary post-war existence. Over

*Anfield, the home of Liverpool Football Club, was surrounded by tightly packed Victorian terraced housing like Kemlyn Rd.*

50,000 people were employed in and around the docks, and football clubs had been nurtured from the communities around them. Post-war Liverpool was a very different place to the modern city we know today. The streets around Anfield were packed with Victorian terraced houses and most fans either walked to the ground or took a tram. There were no floodlights until 1956, so games had to be played during the day – invariably 3pm on a Saturday – and sometimes, if there had been a particularly bad winter like the one of 1946/47, the season would continue into the summer.

Back in those days professional football was a working-class game, and the boot room boys all came from solid, working-class backgrounds – it was the 'people's game'. Not only did the players often live in the same areas as their supporters but the players, coaches and trainers had only slightly better wages than those of the masses that went through the turnstiles. Things were beginning to change, but it would be another 30 years before players' wages, fuelled by television money, would rocket beyond all recognition. After the war, under the leadership of ex-player Jimmy Guthrie, the Professional Footballers' Association threatened to strike for more money, but the players' union were granted a £12 maximum wage during the playing season (£10 in summer) and a minimum wage of £7 for players over 20. The players and their representatives had seen the growing popularity of the mass media and the new phenomenon that was about to sweep the nation – television!

*Ronnie Moran watching television with his girlfriend Joyce in 1955.*

In the post-war period people who couldn't make it to the match would have to listen to the football scores on BBC Radio, huddled around 'the wireless', as only the very rich could afford televisions at that time. In 1948, when the Olympic Games were held in London, the BBC broadcast pictures to only about 100,000 households in the UK, while nearly 9 million held radio licences. A consumer phenomenon was just around the corner.

## 'Shankly would revolutionise Liverpool FC and turn a sleeping giant into a European force.'

As salaries rose in the 1950s, people had more disposable income, so football crowds increased, while the popularity of other leisure activities also grew. Aintree would draw large crowds, and not just for the Grand National steeplechase: over 100,000 people would regularly attend the racecourse to see motor racing. Stirling Moss won the British Grand Prix there in 1955 in front of a crowd of 125,000, a record for a British sporting event at the time.

In the 1950s televisions became the No. 1 'must have' household item. Significantly they became more affordable, so the number owning them rose from 1.5 million in 1951 to 9 million by 1959. My dad told me that in 1953 he travelled several miles from Anfield, where he lived, to watch the Blackpool v Bolton FA Cup Final, also known as the Stanley Matthews Final, which Blackpool won 4-3. A relative had hired a TV with a 12-inch screen that caused a lot of excitement in the family – everyone wanted to see this innovative new device. It was the first televised FA Cup Final, which proved so popular that from then on Cup Finals were broadcast live, as was the final of the 1954 World Cup held in Switzerland.

There were no souvenir shops, so if you wanted to show your dedication to the team by sporting your team's colours, you would have to get someone to knit you a scarf or bobble hat, and with wool being in short supply due to rationing, it would certainly be very expensive.

The success of the boot room was arguably down to the unique bond between a group of men who simply loved the game. They were obsessed with football. It was their life. They did it for the glory of the club, and money didn't really come into it. It was all about the team, the team, and the team!

The boot room really began with the arrival of Bill Shankly in December 1959 and would last nearly 40 years until the departure of Roy Evans in 1998. It was a spiritual place and, like the Liver Birds at the Pier Head, steeped in mystery, mythology and intrigue. Graeme Souness is often blamed for the dismantling of the boot room in 1992, while in reality it was the increasing importance of television and the request for improved media facilities which brought about its physical

*When radio was king. Reuben Bennett, coach, Bill Barlow, assistant secretary, Bob Paisley and Bill Shankly listen to the FA Cup draw 1963.*

demise. But the boot room was never really about a place; it was never about bricks and mortar. It was about an alliance of people who had a common goal, common values and the people who created the philosophy of Liverpool Football Club – the people who created the Liverpool Way.

*Liverpool fans sporting bobble hats and scarves invade the pitch and surround Billy Liddell at Southend in an FA Cup replay held on Wednesday afternoon, 8 January 1958 – Liverpool won 3–2.*

# Chapter 1

## The Birth of the Boot Room

# The Birth of the Boot Room

'They were honest, hard working, loyal and fanatical about football, to the point of obsession.'

It was a small room with no natural light, the distinctive smell of liniment and wet leather football boots hanging on the wall, but for decades it was the nerve centre of Anfield, the think tank of Liverpool Football Club. The boot room has become a part of Liverpool FC's folklore and is cited as the reason behind the club's unprecedented success from the 1960s to the 1990s. Within those walls future managers served their apprenticeship and found their way.

The boot room boys were a highly dedicated and hard-working bunch of men who were devoted to the game and didn't suffer fools gladly. Opposition managers were invited in after matches, but Liverpool players were apparently reluctant to even knock on the door in case they felt the sharp tongue of the occupants. This inner sanctum served Liverpool Football Club well, but it was the individuals who made up the boot room that made it special. Bill Shankly – who rarely ventured into the room itself – encouraged his trusted lieutenants to discuss all aspects of the playing staff and opposition in there. Bob Paisley, Reuben Bennett, Joe Fagan and Ronnie Moran were all at Liverpool when Shankly arrived in December 1959. They were all from a similar background to Bill Shankly: honest, loyal, industrious and fanatical about football, to the point of obsession. They were the backbone that helped Shankly transform Liverpool Football Club into 'a bastion of invincibility'.

In order to understand what made the boot room so special, we need to look into the background of the individuals concerned,

*The Kop roof under construction in 1928.*

and how Liverpool FC emerged from Second Division mediocrity to become a club that would dominate European football for over a decade. Under the inspirational leadership of Bill Shankly and the boot room's collective effort, the club was transformed beyond all recognition. Nobody could have envisaged the possibility of that happening when Bill Shankly arrived to find a dilapidated ground and a training ground with no running water. The lack of investment in the infrastructure of the facilities was matched by the club's lack of investment on the playing field. Supporters from that era remember a club with little or no ambition that was quite happy as long as the gates were healthy. During the 1950s the club was in decline, and

Liverpool as a city was also going through a period of uncertainty. The population of the city – which had peaked in 1931 at 846,000 – was also falling. The bombing of the docks in the Second World War had laid waste to vast areas of the city. Liverpool was going through a vast transformation with tens of thousands being moved out of the city to new estates on the outskirts. Anfield, however, was still surrounded by rows and rows of Victorian terraced houses, which in later years would prove problematic as the directors of the club attempted to expand the ground. In fact the ground had changed very little since the addition of the Kop roof in the 1920s.

*Apart from the addition of the roof Anfield had changed little over the decades since the Kop was built in 1906 – and terraced houses surrounded the ground. Here we can see the old Kop and the Kemlyn Road*

Liverpool Football Club are now one of the most successful football clubs in the world, having won 5 European Cups, 18 League titles and 7 FA Cups. They are certainly one of the most famous clubs, with a massive global fan base, and are also one of the top ten richest clubs with a turnover running into the hundreds of millions of pounds. On any level, they are a massive club, which in the 1950s would have been unthinkable. Back then, Liverpool Football Club were truly in the doldrums, having spent the majority of the decade in the second tier of domestic football.

To understand how Bill Shankly – with the help of the boot room – turned Liverpool into a European force in the 1960s and 1970s, we must first look back to the immediate post-war period. The Football League programme resumed in 1946, over a year after the end of hostilities. Liverpool, under the stewardship of manager George Kay, were triumphant that season, winning the Championship in June 1947. The popular George Kay was regarded as a good motivator and deep thinker. He was always impeccably dressed – never seen in a tracksuit; he was an 'old school manager' if ever there was one.

The league programme had been prolonged due to the harsh winter and numerous postponements. Winning the title was a remarkable achievement, and reports at the time put it down to the tour of the United States of America and Canada the previous summer. Post-war austerity at home meant that even footballers had to tighten their belts. But in North America, where high protein food was not rationed and readily available, the players were able to gain weight and strength. The decision to tour the USA and Canada had been taken by chairman Bill McConnell, who was a successful local caterer with a string of cafés in the city, and he was also very interested in nutrition, which was visionary for those times. After discussions with the manager, he organised a ground-breaking ten-match tour. The players were delighted to escape a country where almost everything was subject to post-war rationing. From the time they left on the *Queen Mary* to their return, one player remarked, 'All we did was eat.' The *New York Times* reported that players, on average, had put on seven pounds during their stay in North America.

Strengthened on and off the field with the addition of forward Albert Stubbins from Newcastle, they went on to win the League after a rollercoaster season. They actually won the trophy in the middle of June 1947, when Stoke failed to win their last game against Sheffield United at Bramall Lane. Liverpool were playing Everton in

*Liverpool players relaxing during their 1946 summer tour of the USA.*

*Liverpool fans queue in the Kop to buy tickets for the FA Cup tie against rivals Everton.*

the Liverpool Senior Cup at the time, so when the news was broadcast over the loudspeakers at the end of the game there was pandemonium, with crowds swarming all over the pitch to carry the League winners off the field.

Shortly after the triumph Bill McConnell was taken ill and died, which was a great shock to everyone at the club.

Liverpool would not reach those heights again for many years. They did manage to reach the 1950 Cup Final but were defeated 2–0 by a resurgent Arsenal, even though they had beaten them twice in the League that season.

The FA Cup Final defeat was a terrible blow for supporters, who started to think they would never win the coveted trophy. The team selection for the final had also been a disappointment for future boot room boy Bob Paisley. Although he was the semi-final hero, having scored the winner at Maine Road against Everton, he was left out of the team for the final. The manager George Kay reportedly wanted to keep him in the team, even though regular midfielder Bill Jones was back from injury, but the board of directors outvoted him.

THE FOOTBALL ASSOCIATION CHALLENGE CUP COMPETITION
**FINAL TIE**
Arsenal v Liverpool
SATURDAY, APRIL 29th, 1950 at 3 pm

OFFICIAL PROGRAMME · ONE SHILLING
The Empire Stadium
**WEMBLEY**

Bob Paisley was distraught at being left out of the Cup Final team, but it would be valuable experience for his future roles at the club. After this setback, George Kay's health continued to deteriorate, and he retired in 1951. Liverpool were on the lookout for a new manager.

In 1951 Bill Shankly unsuccessfully applied for the vacant manager's post. Contrary to popular myth, he didn't turn Liverpool down, but reportedly told the directors that only the manager should pick the team. This obviously didn't impress the board, because it was the Brighton manager (and ex-Charlton player) Don Welsh who was eventually appointed to revive their fortunes.

Welsh inherited a team who included the outstanding Billy Liddell and stalwarts like Bob Paisley, Phil Taylor, Laurie Hughes and Eddie Spicer. But in his first full season, 1951/52, they finished 11th and started a slow, agonising decline. It was a real shame for the likes of Billy Liddell, who spent most of his prime in the second tier. Liddell

*Billy Liddell fires a header towards the Manchester City goal, January 1953.*

was the Liverpool superstar of his day, making 537 appearances and scoring 229 goals. The board weren't too worried, however, as the average gate at Anfield in 1952 was still a healthy 40,000.

With Liverpool FC's form in the League spiralling downwards, they were knocked out of the Cup in January 1953 by Third Division

*Don Welsh talking tactics to the Liverpool team, 10 January 1952. Left to right: Crossley, Liddell, Paisley, Hughes, Payne, Jones and Taylor.*

Gateshead in front of just 15,000 fans. It was only a 2–0 victory against Chelsea in the last League game of the season that saved them from the drop and they finished 17th. But the celebrations of staying up were short-lived. Even though Welsh brought in players such as Geoff Twentyman, from Carlisle, and goalkeeper Dave Underwood, from Watford, he couldn't halt the slide and in 1954, after a disastrous season, Liverpool were relegated, for the first time in 50 years.

Many thought the club would bounce straight back into the First Division, but it wasn't to be. Liverpool was regarded as a well-run club who had never sacked a manager, but it was becoming clear that the board's decision to appoint Don Welsh manager had been a mistake.

Back in 1905, Liverpool had been promoted straight away after just

*Liverpool team training. Left to right: Joe Cadden, Billy Liddell, Jack Balmer, Phil Taylor, Jimmy Payne and Bob Paisley.*

one year in the Second Division, and even went on to win the First Division in their first year back. This relegation was a very different story, and Liverpool would spend eight long years out of the top flight. They were a club in decline, and the fact that they had never won the FA Cup was a source of great amusement to their rivals Everton across Stanley Park. Liverpool's gates at Anfield held up, though, and there was massive demand for tickets when Liverpool were drawn against Everton in the FA Cup in January 1955.

Behind the scenes, meanwhile, through chance, fate and an element of luck, the seeds of the boot room were already being sown. In 1954 Bob Paisley, who had been a loyal servant to the club, was asked to become the reserve team manager, and their form began to improve. This was noted in the boardroom.

When Don Welsh was sacked at the end of the 1955/56 season (the first manager in the history of the club to have suffered this fate), he was replaced as manager by Phil Taylor, and Bob Paisley was made chief coach. Phil Taylor had made 312 appearances for the Reds as a player, and had captained the team until his retirement in 1954. Taylor, who had led Liverpool out in the FA Cup Final in 1950, was determined to get Liverpool back where they belonged.

'The ex-army instructor was a very popular figure with players, even though he worked them very hard and demanded 100 per cent effort.'

Under Taylor, both Reuben Bennett and Joe Fagan were recruited onto the staff. Reuben Bennett arrived at Anfield in 1958, a year before Bill Shankly was appointed, when Phil Taylor was struggling to get Liverpool promoted. The chairman T.V. Williams had heard of his reputation as a coach and was determined to get him to Anfield to help Taylor. Reuben Bennett is often overlooked when it comes to the boot room; although he preferred to stay in the background he was an integral part of the set-up – in many ways he was the unofficial 'enforcer'.

Born in Aberdeen, Reuben Bennett had played in goal for Hull City, Queen of the South, Dundee and finally Elgin. The tough Scotsman moved into management with Ayr United, but after disappointing results over two seasons he moved into coaching. He was not really suited to management but started gaining a tremendous reputation as a coach with Motherwell and Third Lanark, managed by Bill Shankly's brother Bob. The ex-army instructor was a very popular figure with players, even though he worked them very hard and demanded 100 per cent effort, even during training. When Bill Shankly took over in December 1959, he would have been told by his brother Bob about Reuben's ruthless determination to make his players the fittest in the land. Shankly would later describe him as the 'hardest man in the world'.

*Reuben Bennett arriving at Anfield in 1958.*

*Joe Fagan in his early days at Anfield.*

Liverpool-born Joe Fagan had spent most of his career playing for Manchester City as a centre-half, and was actually recommended to Phil Taylor by Harry Catterick, the future Everton manager. During Catterick's managerial stint at Rochdale he had been impressed by Fagan's coaching there. After spending some time as an assistant manager at Rochdale, Fagan was asked to join the staff at Anfield in June 1958, and he took up residence near the ground.

In many ways the straight-talking Scouser was instrumental in the setting up of the boot room. He used to coach the Guinness brewery team and as a thank you they would send him crates of the black stuff. With nowhere else to store them, they would end up in the boot room. His endless supply of Guinness was offered to the guests – and he would always be welcoming to opposing managers. He was quiet and down-to-earth, but many journalists thought he was the brains behind the boot room and he undoubtedly became a vital cog in the success story. Many of the players and coaching staff regarded him as 'the thinker'. Reuben Bennett may have been the taskmaster, but Joe was the quiet strategist. If he ever raised his voice – which wasn't often – people would listen. He was a very private family man, ideally suited to the ethos of the inner sanctum. He was loyal, dedicated and above all honest. If players had a problem they would invariably go to 'Uncle Joe'. Shankly had been a big admirer of Joe Fagan as a player when Shankly was managing Grimsby Town, and had even tried to buy him. Now his straightforward approach and vast knowledge of the game would help Shankly transform Liverpool Football Club beyond all recognition.

Another figure that preceded Bill Shankly was Albert Shelley. I knew the name Albert Shelley from an early age, as his son Ray Shelley used to work with my dad, so we would regularly get tickets

for Liverpool matches off him. My dad had a season ticket but if he wanted to take me as a youngster, Albert Shelley would get us a couple of tickets for the Main Stand. I never actually met him, but he was able to get me Bill Shankly's autograph along with those of the rest of the team.

Shelley was a legendary figure around Anfield, and even after he retired he would still be there every day doing odd jobs, never asking for money. There were always things to be done around the ground and boots to be repaired.

Whether or not he realised it at the time, Shankly was joining a community that regarded ex-employees – players and coaches alike – as part of an extended family. Shelley retired before Shankly arrived, but he was ever present in and around Anfield throughout Shankly's early days. Having been a player and then a trainer at Southampton, Shelley had moved to Anfield in 1937, where he was part of George Kay's coaching staff that won the League after the war. All these various characters were extremely loyal to Liverpool Football Club, but under the management of Phil Taylor their collective effort couldn't turn the team's fortunes around. They needed a leader, they needed a visionary, they needed a force of nature – they needed Bill Shankly!

After five long years in the Second Division they appointed a man who would transform the club and start a red revolution – nothing would be the same again. Whether or not the chairman T.V. Williams and his fellow board members knew what they were getting is debatable. Bill Shankly hadn't been particularly successful with the teams he had managed in the previous ten years, but his appointment to manage Liverpool FC in December 1959 was the catalyst for the transformation of the club. The boot room era was born.

On 17 October 1959, which will always be remembered as a pivotal day in the history of Liverpool Football Club, chairman T.V. Williams and director Harry Latham travelled to Leeds Road, Huddersfield Town's ground, to approach Bill Shankly to become manager. In fact Huddersfield lost that day to Cardiff City, and it would be several weeks before Shankly accepted the post, once he had received

*Liverpool chairman T.V. Williams.*

Right *Shankly's appointment barely made the papers, let alone the headlines. It only warranted a short line above an advert.*

guarantees that he alone would pick the team. It was as if Shankly had been preparing himself all these years to take charge of a club that he knew had huge potential. Even though Huddersfield had beaten Liverpool the previous season 5-0, Shankly knew that the Leeds Road directors lacked ambition and kept on selling their best players. Shankly had experience of playing at Anfield and he knew the city had a very similar feel to Glasgow. He had been to watch Celtic and Rangers many times but had no time for the sectarian rivalries – he just wanted to watch as many games as possible.

There was a general perception among Liverpool supporters that the directors of the club were quite happy to be challenging for promotion, rather than actually trying to achieve it, as long as they were attracting healthy gates. If they thought Bill Shankly was a safe pair of hands to continue the status quo, they were very much mistaken. Shankly was a human whirlwind, propelled by his own natural enthusiasm and belief in his own abilities as a manager and in the collective endeavour of his staff and players.

On 1 December 1959, Bill Shankly was appointed to take over from Phil Taylor as manager of Liverpool Football Club without any great fanfare; it warranted only a couple of lines in the *Daily Mirror*. Taylor had retired the previous month, exhausted by his efforts to gain promotion over four seasons. Fans had become disillusioned with the club and a general air of apathy hung over Anfield. Nobody but nobody could foresee what was coming. After touring the ground, Shankly was astounded at the dilapidated state of Anfield. He had visited the ground previously, but on closer inspection declared it to be the 'biggest toilet in Liverpool'. He knew the supporters were desperate for a miracle to transform the club's fortunes and he was determined to provide it. He immediately set about improving the facilities, with all hands to the pump – literally, as facilities to water the pitches at Anfield and Melwood were non-existent. The first thing Shankly did was make the water flow – the red revolution was about to begin!

*Paisley, Bennett, Shankly, Fagan.*

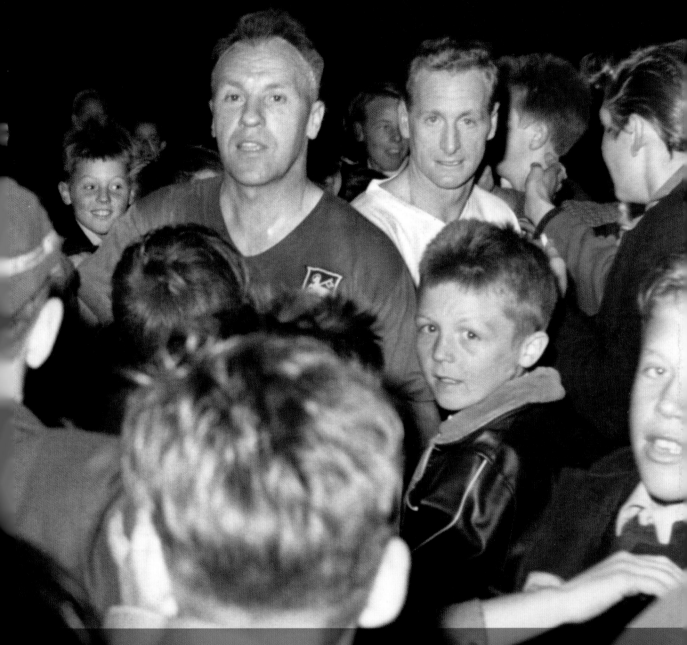

# Chapter 2

## The Arrival

*Preston North End, FA Cup winners in 1938. Back row (left to right): Bill Shankly, Len Gallimore, William Scott (trainer), George Holdcroft, Andy Beattie, Bob Batey. Front row: Bud Maxwell, Robert Beattie, George Mutch, Tom Smith (captain), Dickie Watmough, Hugh O'Donnell.*

# The Arrival

Bill Shankly was born in Glenbuck, Ayrshire, 20 miles south of Glasgow, in 1913. He was the second youngest of ten children, five brothers and five sisters. His uncles on his mother's side had been professional footballers: Robert Blyth had played for Glasgow Rangers and Portsmouth, and William Blyth had played for Preston North End and Carlisle. Nobody in the village was very surprised when all five Shankly brothers became professional footballers; it was in their blood. The Shankly family lived and breathed football, as did many of their fellow 'Glenbuckians'. They would play as often as they could in the streets or Burnside Park, and it was not unusual for games to be 20-a-side. The winter months were often savage and unforgiving in Ayrshire, but in the summer months these kickabouts could last well into the night – until it was too dark.

Shankly's belief in communal spirit and collective endeavour was undoubtedly nurtured in his hometown mining community. It was a solid working-class area with a history of solidarity and trade unionism. Shankly had worked hard in the mines from the age of 14, when he left school, but he was obsessed with football and preferred the fresh air and open fields of the village. His reputation grew as he played for the local team Cronberry, and soon scouts watching him alerted both Carlisle and Preston to his talent. At the age of 17 he went on a month's trial to Carlisle but impressed so much that they signed him after just one game. He would never need to go down a mine again.

Shankly saw Carlisle as a stepping-stone to bigger things, and he was right. After one season he was snapped up by Second Division Preston, who had been keeping a close eye on him throughout his season at Carlisle. He signed for £500 in 1933 for a weekly wage of £5 – not much more than he was getting at Carlisle, but after advice from his brothers he made the move. He helped Preston gain promotion to the First Division in 1934 and win the FA Cup in 1938 as well as gaining 12 caps for Scotland. The Preston years finely tuned his footballing philosophy that would serve him so well in his days at Anfield.

Bill Shankly said that he saw his days at Deepdale as preparation for his future career move into management. His self-belief and ability to motivate would soon be put to the test when the Carlisle manager's job became vacant. His Uncle Bill was a director there, and he applied for the job and was successful. Preston team-mate and close friend Tom Finney urged him to stay, but Shankly knew that at the age of 35 his playing days were numbered.

It was the start of a new challenge for Shankly, but he was confident that he had the qualities to succeed. When he moved to Carlisle he claimed to be 'as fit as anyone in England'. At Carlisle, he claimed he did everything: training, practice matches, scouting, even cleaning the boots and the dressing-rooms. The team were playing in front of decent crowds averaging 17,000, and Shankly said he tried to show that the fans were the people who really mattered. This would become his blueprint for all the clubs he managed.

When Shankly arrived at Carlisle he immediately changed the way they trained. He made sure training was hard but also enjoyable, with the emphasis on ball work. In his first full season in charge, Carlisle

*Bill Shankly* (far right) *as manager of Carlisle in 1951 with Geoff Twentyman* (third from the right), *who would be an important part of the boot room in their Liverpool years – Twentyman remembers Shankly saying, 'We play on grass, you train on grass.'*

finished ninth in the Third Division North and the following season only just missed out on promotion, finishing third. Shankly was convinced that with the club's coffers swelled by a decent FA Cup run – including a game against Arsenal at Highbury – the directors would invest in the squad to help with his push for promotion, but funds weren't forthcoming.

After a disagreement with the Carlisle board over player bonuses, Shankly moved to Grimsby Town in June 1951 (but only after an unsuccessful interview with Liverpool FC). Officially he said he thought Grimsby had more potential than Carlisle, but his decision may well have been influenced by the fact that he thought Carlisle just didn't have the money to progress. In his first season at Grimsby – 1951/52 – they just missed out on promotion, but Shankly felt that that pound-for-pound and class-for-class, they were the best football team in England since the war. It was at Grimsby that he saw the real

> **'Shankly would spend much of his time with the groundsman Billy Watson in the boiler-room, one of the few warm places in the ground.'**

importance of five-a-side games in training that would come to the fore during his time at Anfield.

If Shankly thought there was more potential at Grimsby, it was an illusion. After two disappointing seasons with an ageing squad that he thought wouldn't even be improved by new signings, he was on the move again. Workington – who were also in the Third Division North and struggling – approached him mid-season to reverse their fortunes. It was January 1954 and Shankly had certainly taken a step down in managerial terms, as the facilities at Workington's Borough Park were archaic compared to Grimsby's, but he threw himself into the job with all the enthusiasm he could muster. Instilling discipline into the team and using his tried and trusted training methods, Shankly reversed their fortunes immediately and relegation was avoided.

With money at the club scarce, Shankly helped with nearly everything. In between training, answering the phone and sorting out the players' wages, he would spend much of his time with the groundsman Billy Watson in the boiler-room, one of the few warm places in the ground. They would sit and discuss football over endless cups of tea.

In the close season after the great escape the directors agreed to invest money in players, and even modernised the dressing rooms. Shankly's new training scheme and methods, coupled with the arrival of new players, began to reap rewards and Workington finished in eighth place. The following season, the players and staff were forced to take a wage cut due to cash problems, and Shankly had to rely upon bringing youngsters into the team. Things weren't looking good for him until an old friend from his Preston days, Andy Beattie, who was by then the manager of Huddersfield, got in touch asking him to play in a testimonial game at Huddersfield under their new floodlights. Andy Beattie confided in Shankly that he was struggling at Leeds Road and was looking for an assistant. Shankly jumped at the chance: it was another calculated risk and another massive challenge, as Huddersfield were rooted to the bottom of the First Division. Workington's directors were disappointed, but the parting wasn't acrimonious as Shankly had made many friends there and they appreciated all his hard work. It was December 1955 and 'Rock Around the Clock' by Bill Haley and His Comets had just stormed to the top of the UK charts. The times were changing.

Shankly took over the reserve team at Huddersfield and impressed by giving youngsters a chance. After the first team were relegated in 1956, Andy Beattie resigned and Shankly was offered the job as manager on 5 November 1956. Like elsewhere, as soon as he took charge, the atmosphere in the dressing room changed. Whereas the unapproachable Beattie had been somewhat of a disciplinarian, Shankly was the complete opposite. From now on the manager's door

*Bill Shankly coaching young Huddersfield players during a 1959 training session.*

would always be open. Shankly's reign at Leeds Road was hardly spectacular, though; over 129 games his win rate was only 38 per cent. Similar to his spells at Carlisle, Grimsby and Workington, it was a rollercoaster of hope and despair. He was giving young players like Denis Law and Ray Wilson a chance, but at the back of his mind he always felt the board didn't share his vision.

A familiar pattern was beginning to emerge – as a football obsessive Shankly wanted success, but his ambition wasn't shared by the cautious 'businessmen' who ran the club. He looked admiringly at the side his old team-mates and friends Matt Busby and ex-Carlisle trainer Tom Curry were developing at Manchester United. Tragically, halfway through the 1957/58 season the football world was shaken by news of the Munich Air Disaster on 6 February. There were 23 fatalities, including 8 Manchester United players and 3 staff. Tom Curry was among the dead. Matt Busby, the manager of Manchester United, survived the crash but football was in mourning. Shankly was devastated.

After the initial shock, Shankly continued to put all his energy into producing a team that could compete. In his first full season in charge, Huddersfield finished a disappointing ninth, and the following season the Terriers could only finish fourteenth. Significantly, their best result was a 5-0 win against Liverpool in October 1958 – fate was beginning to play its hand. In his autobiography Shankly remembers the Liverpool directors after the thrashing 'leaving the ground in single file, their shoulders slumped like a funeral procession'. One thing is certain: Shankly had made a lasting impression on the Liverpool board, especially the chairman T.V. Williams.

The Liverpool chairman had been keeping a close eye on Shankly's Huddersfield team, and was impressed with his mix of established players and youngsters like Denis Law and Ray Wilson. Shankly meanwhile was getting frustrated at the lack of ambition at Leeds Road. He went to see fellow Scots Ian St John and Ron Yeats playing against each other in a friendly match in Falkirk and he was convinced they could be the difference between promotion and failure. During board meetings he tried to convince the directors to buy them, but

*Shankly in his office at Leeds Road, Huddersfield.*

*Shankly inspects the Leeds Road pitch with the groundsman and the chairman.*

they said they couldn't afford even one of them, never mind both. Shankly was becoming increasingly disillusioned with the board's lack of foresight. After a promising start to the 1959/60 season, when they looked like genuine promotion candidates, their form suddenly dipped. After losing to Cardiff 1-0 at home on 17 October 1959, a disappointed Shankly was walking towards his car when he noticed two figures in the dusk. T.V. Williams and director Harry Latham approached Shankly and asked him: 'How would you like to manage the best club in the country?' Shankly quipped, 'Why? Is Matt Busby packing up?' It was a typical sharp-witted Shankly response. He agreed to talk it over with his wife Nessie and let them know in due course, but he could see both the potential of Liverpool and the lack of ambition at Huddersfield, so in his heart of hearts he knew immediately he wanted to become Liverpool's manager.

Worcester v Liverpool, January 1959. Liverpool's goalkeeper Tommy Younger collects the ball from a Worcester attack. This cup shock sealed Phil Taylor's fate.

It was several weeks before anything formal was announced, and although Shankly spoke to no one about the offer except his wife, rumours were rife that Liverpool wanted him as their manager. Huddersfield beat Liverpool 1-0 on 28 November, but it wasn't until Shankly delivered his report for the weekly board meeting the following Tuesday that he dropped his bombshell: he had agreed to join Liverpool Football Club. On Monday, 14 December 1959, two weeks after the news of his appointment broke, Bill Shankly took up the position of manager of Liverpool on an annual salary of £2,500. He was 46 years old.

When Bill Shankly arrived at Anfield at the end of 1959, the Cavern Club in Mathew Street had been open as a jazz club for nearly three years but rock and roll bands had started to be booked more frequently. John Lennon was at art college, Paul McCartney had a Christmas job at the Post Office and George Harrison was reluctantly looking into becoming an electrician. All three were playing with a group called the Quarrymen in a club called the Casbah in the West Derby area, a stone's throw from Liverpool's Melwood training ground. BBC *Grandstand* was over a year old, but *Match of the Day* was still several years away. Adam Faith topped the charts with 'What Do You Want?' produced by John Burgess and arranged by John Barry, who would later go on to compose 11 scores for James Bond films. The Hollywood epic *Ben Hur* was just about to get its UK release and would become one of the biggest films in history.

In 1959 redevelopment was taking place on a huge scale and whole areas of Liverpool were being demolished. People were being rehoused in massive outer council estates like Kirkby, Halewood, Speke and Croxteth – the city was transforming beyond all recognition. With the arrival of Bill Shankly, Liverpool Football Club was about to follow suit.

Deep down Shankly knew that there was something special about Liverpool Football Club. He already knew trainers and coaches Bob Paisley, Reuben Bennett and Joe Fagan, and decided that they were the type of men who could help him transform the fortunes of the club. The first thing he did on day one was to have a meeting with

Left to right: *Johnny Morrissey, Geoff Twentyman and Gerry Byrne, 1959.*

them and reassure them that while he would lay down the plans, they would help him fulfil those plans, with them all working in harmony. The one thing that Shankly demanded was loyalty. 'I don't want people to carry stories about anybody else ... if anybody tells me a story about someone else, the man with the story will get the sack. I don't care if he's been here fifty years. I want everyone to be loyal to each other. Everything we do will be for Liverpool Football Club.' The manifesto was in place!

Shankly knew enough about Paisley, Bennett and Fagan to trust and respect them and it's fair to say the feeling was mutual. Shankly then had to assess the playing staff and improve the conditions at Anfield itself and the training ground at Melwood, which was about three and a half miles from Anfield. On the second day in charge he visited Melwood, and found that while it was situated in a picturesque suburb of Liverpool there was nothing pretty about the training

A Second Division match between Stoke City and Liverpool at the Victoria Ground in the 1959/60 season. Stoke's Dennis Wilshaw battles for the ball with Ronnie Moran of Liverpool in the 1-1 draw.

ground. It was a dilapidated eyesore. The wooden hut that passed as a changing room had no heating and there was no hot water. He was shocked and bitterly disappointed at the state of the place, but within a few weeks he started to transform it. Coming from a proud working-class tradition, Shankly wanted the best for his players, and for him cleanliness was next to godliness. He wanted everything spotless.

Within weeks of arriving, Shankly had changed nearly everything to do with training. There had been a tradition of arriving at Anfield then jogging to Melwood for more running, but he soon put a stop to that. Players would still arrive at Anfield but then they would get a coach to Melwood. They played on grass, so Shankly wanted them to train on grass, and he wasn't happy with them running on pavements to Melwood and back.

His first task was to assess the players' and the squad's strengths and weaknesses and to work out what they would need to challenge for promotion. Shankly did this by getting to know his players, training with them, eating with them and speaking to them. He spelled out what he wanted from the players: maximum effort in training and in matches. Shankly and his backroom staff completely reorganised the whole training system. Daily discussions took place between Shankly, Paisley, Bennett and Fagan and every detail was meticulously planned. Each player was different and, according to Shankly, needed his own distinct training schedule. Tactical discussions were integral to the new regime but Shankly believed they should be just that, a discussion, not him talking down to his players. He encouraged

*Shankly inherited a decent squad but he knew he had to improve it if he was to gain promotion from the Second Division where they had been since the 1954/55 season.* Left to right: *Alan A'Court, Ronnie Moran, Roger Hunt, Billy Liddell and Dave Hickson.*

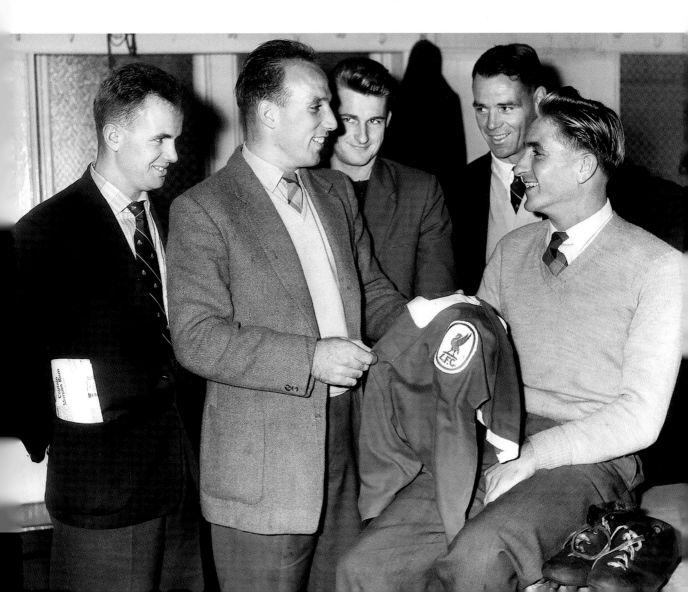

*Bob Paisley, Bill Shankly and Joe Fagan discuss tactics and training methods – Shankly encouraged his boot room boys to express their opinions at every opportunity.*

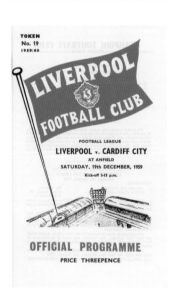

his future boot room boys to express their thoughts and ideas, and he also encouraged players to say what they felt. He knew he had inherited a disillusioned, mediocre team, but he was convinced that the methods he believed in would eventually come good.

Shankly's first match was at home to Cardiff City on 19 December 1959 and it was a massive disappointment. In front of 27,000 people they were beaten 4-0 by a Cardiff outfit pressing for promotion. He could see he had a huge task in front of him. Shankly was a great believer in learning from defeats, and he even told the players when they held a post mortem on the game that the defeat was the best thing that could have happened to them. But he also knew he had to strengthen the team, and he told the directors that to challenge for promotion they needed new blood. In his first half-season in charge, Liverpool finished in third position, eight points off the promotion places. The search for talent was on.

One person who had played under Phil Taylor and continued under Bill Shankly was goalkeeper Tommy Lawrence. Having signed for Liverpool from Warrington Town in October 1957, Lawrence became a regular in Shankly's first brilliant team of the 1960s. In an exclusive interview with Mike Hughes for BBC Radio Merseyside in 2012 Lawrence remembered the Phil Taylor years being 'very easy going' compared to Shankly's regime. Taylor was popular and well liked, but according to Lawrence he was too nice to be a manager. Lawrence, who was in Liverpool's reserve team at the time, said even many of the first team preferred to play for the reserves, on account of the £2 win bonus. He explained that this was because the reserves were always winning, whereas the £4 win bonus for the first team was rare. 'There didn't seem to be any go in anybody at all at that time,' said

*Liverpool v Manchester United in the fourth round of the FA Cup, January 1960. Liverpool lost 3-1 to Matt Busby's team, but the crowd of over 56,000 showed the enormous appetite for football that Shankly already knew about.*

Lawrence. Shankly was the polar opposite of Taylor and the emphasis was on football rather than gruelling ten-mile runs in pre-season training. Lawrence said it took four or five months for Shankly's training to come to fruition and watching them in the 1960/61 season was fantastic, but they still just missed out on promotion, finishing third again. During this period the boot room was in its embryonic stages, but Paisley, Fagan and Bennett were all playing their part in creating what would eventually become Shankly's legacy. Confidence was growing, but to bridge the gap from third to promotion Shankly knew he had to convince a board of directors who didn't share his vision that things needed to change dramatically.

# Chapter 3

Shankly: The Vision

'I am very pleased and proud to have been chosen as manager of Liverpool FC, a club of great potential. It is my opinion that Liverpool have a crowd of followers which rank with the greatest in the game. They deserve success and I hope in my small way to be able to do something towards helping them to achieve it. I make no promises except that from the moment I take over I shall put everything into the job. I am not a lazy man. I like to get down to it and set an example which I will want following from the top of the club to the bottom.'

Bill Shankly, December 1959

# Shankly: The Vision

After that very first match, the 4-0 defeat by Cardiff at Anfield in December 1959, Shankly knew the team was not good enough. He immediately made up his mind that the spine of the team needed strengthening. He had inherited quite a large squad of over 40 players, but he had to streamline the team and then introduce youngsters like Roger Hunt, Gerry Byrne, Ian Callaghan, Tommy Smith and Chris Lawler. Players liked Shankly's new training methods and his emphasis on five-a-side games, and were impressed that he was coaching them rather than simply doing exercises without the ball. Paisley, Fagan and Bennett were keen advocates of the new training methods and everything was now planned meticulously. Shankly based his training methods on the Preston North End model. He said he didn't want marathon runners or circus artists; he wanted footballers. Shankly made a list of 24 players who didn't fit into his 'footballing' plans, but the clear-out was gradual rather than the immediate revolution many players had feared.

*Shankly training at Melwood, October 1961. Left to right: White, Lewis, Hunt, Melia, A'Court.*

Shankly had asked the board if he could snatch Denis Law from Huddersfield, but the directors rejected the idea out of hand as he would be too expensive. Law signed for Manchester City in March 1960 for £65,000 – way above the £18,000 that the Liverpool board were willing to spend. Shankly then made a bold attempt to sign Jack Charlton from Leeds United. He had been following Charlton's progress for years and was convinced that Charlton, at around £20,000, was worth every penny. The Liverpool board were not as convinced and still would not go over their £18,000 limit. Shankly pleaded with chairman T.V. Williams to meet Leeds United's asking price, but the answer was a resounding no. Shankly was furious and started to think the budgetary promises made by Williams and the board to get him to join Liverpool had been a deception.

In the early days Shankly had to fight and argue all the time and, on

'Shankly would often confide in his great friend Matt Busby, who convinced him to stick it out.'

many occasions, he was close to leaving. He would often confide in his great friend Matt Busby, who convinced him to stick it out. At other clubs Shankly had understood their limitations, but at Liverpool things were different. He could see the potential, but he had to convince the directors that they couldn't get talented players on the cheap. He felt the directors were quite happy with things as they stood, as they were getting good gates and were in the top half of the Second Division. However, the fans craved success and a return to the top flight. He compared the directors to gamblers on a losing streak who were 'afraid to bet any more'. But Bill Shankly was a gambler, as he had proved throughout his career. He knew football in the 1960s was moving towards a new era 'when the strong would become stronger and the weak would become weaker'.

It began to dawn on Shankly that, contrary to his belief that there was a £60,000 budget for players, he had really been brought in to achieve stability on a shoestring budget. The board had seen him developing young players at Huddersfield and that was the attraction. Shankly felt betrayed. Local newspaper reporters covering Liverpool FC at the time remember him ranting and raving and threatening to resign. Things had to change.

The 1960/61 season started with some optimism as Liverpool beat the recently relegated Leeds United 2-0 in front of a crowd of 43,000. However, much to the disappointment of the fans and the manager himself, Liverpool hadn't really strengthened in the close season. They had bought Sammy Reid, a winger, from Motherwell for £8,000, but he never actually made an appearance for the club. Shankly's next foray into the transfer market was to sign Kevin Lewis, another winger, from Sheffield United. After the failure of Reid the directors grilled Shankly about his target, but they knew they had to replace Billy Liddell, who was then 38 years old. Shankly once again inquired about Jack

*Gordon Milne signed from Preston North End for £16,000 in August 1960.*

Charlton, and as Leeds had been relegated they were willing to cash in, but the price had gone up to £30,000. The board gave Shankly the same answer as before, telling him that he would have to be less ambitious. Years later this decision would come back to haunt the club as Don Revie built his great Leeds team around the towering defender. Shankly's attention turned to Gordon Milne from his old club Preston North End. He joined in August 1960 for a fee of £16,000 – a club record – but although Milne proved to be a useful midfield asset to the team of the 1960s, he wasn't the domineering centre-back that Shankly craved.

Early optimism turned to gloom as Liverpool lost four of their first eight matches, and by mid-October gates were back down to 25,000. Shankly had left Huddersfield as he thought they lacked ambition and now he was stuck with the very same problem. He looked enviously over to Stanley Park and the ambition of Everton FC. Rivals Everton were regarded as the bigger club in those days and they had the

*Ironically Littlewoods owner and Evertonian John Moores helped create the modern Liverpool FC by appointing Littlewoods executive Eric Sawyer to the Liverpool board of directors to act as his nominee.*

*Bill Shankly with the Liverpool directors.* Back (left to right): *Cecil Hill, Eric Sawyer, Sidney Reakes, Bill Shankly and Tom Smith.* Front: *Eric Roberts and T.V. Williams.*

backing of Littlewoods Pools supremo John Moores. Their manager John Carey was spending money that Shankly could only dream of, buying players like Roy Vernon for £27,000 and Alex Young and George Thomson from Hearts for a combined fee of £55,000.

With the directors starting to interfere in team matters, Shankly truly felt he had been duped into accepting the job. Then something extraordinary happened. Multimillionaire John Moores, who had been a major shareholder in both Liverpool and Everton over the years, had been elected to the Everton board in March 1960. He wanted to take a more active role at Goodison, but he still had a shareholder interest in Liverpool. He couldn't sit on both boards without antagonising the fans of both clubs, so he persuaded the Liverpool board to accept

Eric Sawyer, the financial executive of the Littlewoods organisation, as his nominee. Sawyer was appointed to look after Moores's investment in Liverpool, but Moores as an Evertonian could never have envisaged that this appointment would be the catalyst for Liverpool FC to become the global club it is today, dwarfing Everton, who were known in the 1960s as the 'Mersey millionaires'.

Everything changed the day Eric Sawyer was appointed. At last Shankly had a man who shared his foresight and together they ripped up the club's rule book. It has emerged since that there was a boardroom minute book from the 1950s which stated that the club shouldn't pay more than £12,000 for a player, and that each new signing should be seen by at least two directors and if possible be at least six foot tall. The bureaucracy and outdated policy were suffocating the club and Shankly knew it was now or never.

Shankly must have viewed the directors in much the same way as the coal miners of Glenbuck viewed the pit owners. He wasn't from their world of business, secret handshakes and local government, and he didn't trust them. He certainly didn't trust their views on football and resented having to justify himself all the time to people with a fraction of his footballing knowledge. According to Shankly the appointment of Eric Sawyer was the beginning of Liverpool, as he was willing to spend money. He said to Shankly, 'If you can get the players I will get you the money.' Shankly had many discussions with Sawyer about the players he needed to build the foundations of a successful club, and striker Ian St John (who played for Motherwell) and Ron Yeats (the Dundee United centre-half) were never far from his mind. Then one Sunday morning in 1961 the *Sunday Post* ran the headline 'St John wants to go'. Shankly was on the phone to them and to his new ally on the board Sawyer straight away. Assured by Shankly that St John was the best centre-forward in Scotland, the Littlewoods financier agreed to back Shankly's judgement with the rest of the board, and Shankly arranged to travel to Scotland on the Monday with chairman T.V. Williams and director Sid Reakes. St John signed on 2 May 1961 for £37,500, even after interest from Newcastle, who were a First Division club. St John revealed that Newcastle were offering

*Ian St John playing for Motherwell against Kilmarnock, February 1960.*

more money but when he met Shankly his 'personality, enthusiasm and manner just overwhelmed me. He was so charismatic, he just made you want to play for him.'

With St John's signature secured, attention turned to the centre-half position. Shankly wanted big Ron Yeats from Dundee United, but after spending so much on St John he feared the price tag would prove to be a problem. The board slapped a £20,000 limit on their spending, so an initial trip to Dundee by Shankly, Sawyer and Reakes proved disappointing. Although willing to talk, Dundee United didn't really want to sell Yeats and the player was quite happy there, so they let it be known that they would be looking at £40,000 to tempt them. But as the Liverpool contingent were about to board their train home, Dundee United director Duncan Hutchinson – who had given them a lift back to the station – whispered in Shankly's ear, 'I bet you could get him for £30,000.' All the way back to Liverpool Shankly kept his counsel, as he wanted to convince Eric Sawyer privately that Yeats was the missing piece in the jigsaw. He obviously didn't trust Sid Reakes enough to confide in him. When he was able to speak to Sawyer alone he agreed to talk it over with the board. It took all Sawyer's powers of persuasion, but the directors agreed to go up to £30,000. Shankly, Williams, Reakes and Bennett travelled up to Dundee on Saturday 22 July to finalise the deal. The rule book had been well and truly ripped up!

*In Shankly's view the Ian St John and Ron Yeats signings were the start of everything.*

The signings of St John and Yeats were inspirational. They were both 23, and Shankly was so confident of their quality that he told Eric Sawyer to sack him if they couldn't play well. He also told Sidney Reakes, 'These players will not only win us promotion they will win the Cup as well.' Ron Yeats remembers asking Shankly when they

# 'St John and Yeats had an immediate effect after years of mediocrity.'

first met, 'Whereabouts in England is Liverpool?' As quick as a flash Shankly replied, 'What do you mean, where's Liverpool? We're in the First Division in England, son.' Yeats, who had meant what part of England Liverpool was located in, replied, 'Oh, I thought you were in the Second Division,' to which Shankly answered, 'We are at the moment but with you in the side we will soon be in the First Division.' Like St John, Yeats was bowled over by Shankly's personality. He had been happy at Dundee United and might even have stayed there had they offered him a wage increase, but Shankly's enthusiasm to sign him meant the question was never asked.

The signings of St John and Yeats, which Shankly said were 'the start of it all', had an immediate effect on the red half of the city and,

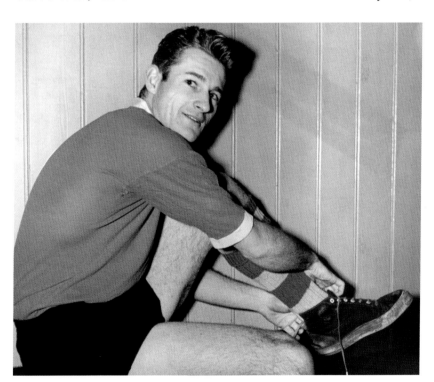

*Roger Hunt, March 1962.*

after years of mediocrity and disappointment, enthusiasm for the coming season was palpable. The signings had excited Liverpudlians so much so that nearly 49,000 turned up to the first home match of the 1961/62 season against Sunderland – in stark contrast to the 13,389 who had seen the last home game of the previous

*Ian St John and Reuben Bennett
lead the squad in training.*

season against Stoke City. It had taken Shankly over 18 months to
assemble a team that would ignite the supporters. There had been
many arguments along the way, and he had considered walking out
on numerous occasions, but with his ally Eric Sawyer supporting
Shankly's vision in the boardroom, the supporters started to believe in
the club.

With St John and Yeats in the team, at the beginning of the 1961/62
season Liverpool won their first six games in a row and went top
of the table. Shankly kept the nucleus of the winning team together
throughout the season with just the odd change here and there, such
as Gerry Byrne moving to right back from the left. Shankly's two
signings galvanised the rest of the team and none more so than the

*Morrissey, Hunt, A'Court, Melia and St John, 1962.*

young Roger Hunt, who scored an incredible 41 goals in 41 games that season including five hat-tricks. In the previous season he had scored 15 in 32 games. St John's presence and energy had given Hunt more time and space and the attacking style introduced by Shankly suited him perfectly. St John also scored 18 goals as the pair developed a lethal partnership that propelled Liverpool into the First Division. Ron Yeats – who had been made captain – was magnificent at the back and Liverpool won the League by eight points ahead of Leyton Orient. Liverpool had a decent run in the FA Cup too, beating Chelsea 4-3 at Anfield, then Oldham away, before eventually going out to Shankly's old team Preston North End after two replays.

Liverpool stayed top of the League throughout that season, playing some magnificent football and scoring 99 goals. They secured promotion on 21 April 1962 with a 2-0 win against Southampton. Reporter Michael Charters wrote later in the *Liverpool Echo*: 'The skies wept, the atmosphere was grey and dismal, but it was still a glorious unforgettable day at Anfield on Saturday.' Thousands invaded the pitch and wouldn't leave the ground until there was a second lap of honour after the players had changed. Long after the players had headed down the tunnel, ceaseless chants of 'We want the Reds!' brought them back again. Singing at football matches was unusual in those days but the Liverpool crowd were ahead of the game and

*Left Liverpool players leave the pitch after winning the Second Division.*

*Right Ron Yeats is mobbed as he attempts a lap of honour. One of the youngsters on the pitch was a young Roy Evans who would later play for Liverpool before becoming one of the boot room boys.*

this was the first time anyone can remember it happening en masse and with such enthusiasm. T.V. Williams and Shankly both addressed the crowd on the public address system but they could hardly be heard over the noise of the crowd. Williams said they had just won the hardest thing in football and Shankly declared it was the proudest moment of his life so far. 'Immediately the crowd swarmed onto the pitch,' wrote Charters. 'Yeats and St John were submerged under the backslapping, kissing, wildly enthusiastic mob. The rest of the team, from the top step leading to the pitch, took one look and disappeared back.'

Charters added: 'A final thought on the season from Mr Shankly. He said: "We won the championship in the first month when we were fitter competitively than our rivals. We beat Sunderland and Newcastle twice in that spell and we never looked back." So it's First Division ahead and Liverpool have the spirit and confidence to make their mark there too.' Michael Charters could not have known how prophetic

these words would turn out to be over the following decades.

Not only had Shankly smashed through the club's signing-on fee ceiling, transformed the training methods and convinced the directors to improve antiquated Anfield and Melwood; he had also introduced a policy of watching Liverpool's opponents. In modern times this doesn't seem extraordinary but, in those days, it was almost unheard of. Shankly sent his trusted lieutenants of the boot room to assess the strengths and weaknesses of coming opponents.

Shankly had upset a few people at the club along the way, but he was so confident that he was doing the right thing for the future of the club that he carried on regardless. In the interviews he gave after promotion he was keen to thank his back room staff. Shankly stated in a *Liverpool Echo* interview that 'without the help of Reuben Bennett, Joe Fagan, Albert Shelley and Bob Paisley we could have achieved nothing. No praise can be too high for these men who have worked so hard and who normally receive no public recognition.' The boot room was born, and Shankly was well and truly closing the door on the past and opening the door for a glorious future.

Above and right: *Joe Richards, president of the Football League, presents Ron Yeats with the Second Division trophy.*

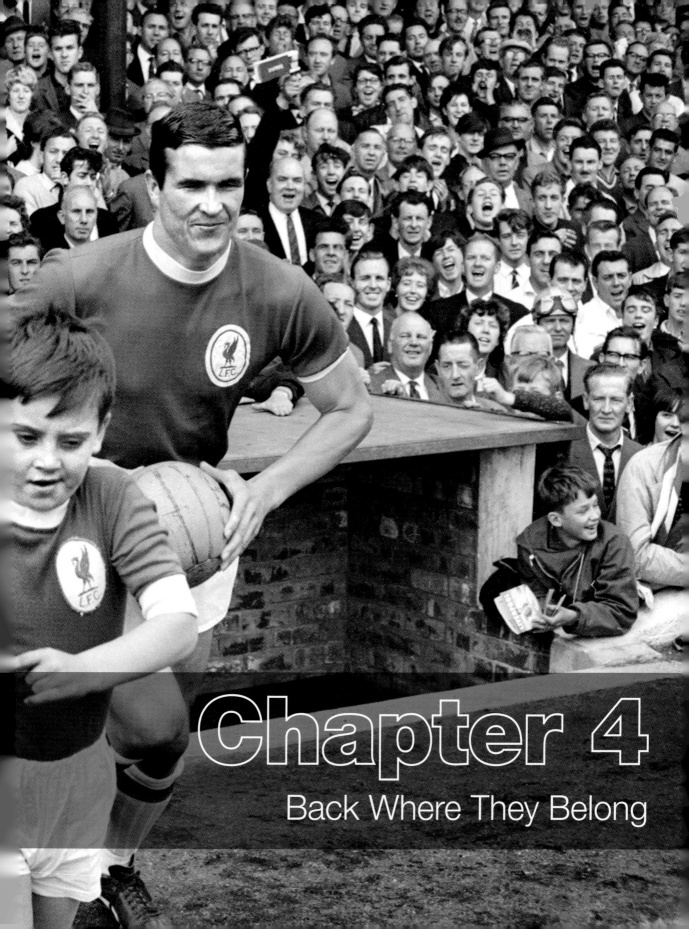

# Chapter 4

Back Where They Belong

*The Liverpool squad at the start of the 1962/63 season.* Back row (left to right): Gordon Milne, Gerry Byrne, Tommy Leishman, Jim Furnell, Tommy Lawrence, Ron Yeats, Ronnie Moran. Centre row: Kevin Lewis, Roger Hunt, Ian St John, Jimmy Melia, Alan A'Court. Front row: Allan Jones, Alf Arrowsmith, Johnny Morrissey, Ian Callaghan.

# Back Where They Belong

After promotion in 1962, Shankly knew he had to improve the team to compete in the top tier. He certainly wasn't expecting the Liverpool board to sell winger Johnny Morrissey without his approval. Although Morrissey hadn't appeared at all in the previous season, Shankly didn't want to sell him, and had a furious row with the board in August 1962. Eventually he had to accept the deal, but let he them know in no uncertain terms that if they ever tried to sell a player without his approval again he would resign.

Liverpool's first game back in Division One was against Blackpool in front of 51,000, which they lost 2-1. Then, after travelling to Manchester City, where they drew 2-2, they lost away to Blackburn. Two home wins improved their League position, but Shankly could see that Liverpool were struggling and he knew he had to change things if they were going to compete. He certainly had a soft spot for his promotion side, but he also knew the time for sentiment was over. After lengthy discussions with his boot room he decided to bring midfielder Willie Stevenson in from Rangers for £20,000 to replace midfielder Tommy Leishman, who was struggling in the First Division.

Stevenson was a stylish, intelligent midfielder and epitomised the type of player Shankly and the boot room wanted. He also gave goalkeeper Tommy Lawrence his debut in October 1962 when regular goalkeeper Jim Furnell was injured.

The changes strengthened the side with immediate effect and Liverpool put together an impressive nine consecutive wins from November 1962 to March 1963. Furnell and Leishman wouldn't regain their places and Tommy Lawrence, who had been at the club

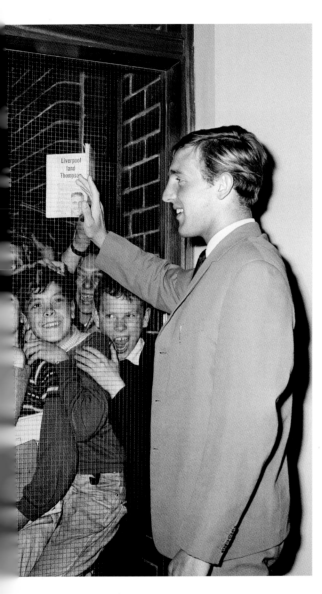

*Peter Thompson was pursued by all the top clubs, and when he signed for Liverpool, Thompson-mania erupted!*

since 1957 and had come through the ranks, would make the goalkeeping position his own for the next eight years. The impressive winter run was a sign of things to come, even if the poor start to the season meant Liverpool could only finish eighth. The team was certainly taking shape. The spine of the team – Lawrence, Yeats and St John – had been established, while Hunt, Milne, Callaghan, Byrne and new signing Stevenson had become regulars. Youngsters like Tommy Smith and Chris Lawler were also pushing for a first-team place, but Shankly still wanted to improve the side in order to push for silverware.

Peter Thompson was the man Shankly identified as the missing piece of the jigsaw. Thompson was a skilful left-footed winger who could glide past defenders, and Shankly later said that getting him from Preston North End for just £37,000 was 'daylight robbery'.

With young Ian Callaghan on the right wing and Peter Thompson on the left supplying crosses for Hunt and St John, Liverpool were finally ready to challenge for honours. The Liverpool board didn't baulk at the cost as Shankly had finally convinced even the most pessimistic of them that he was building a team that could win trophies. Shankly also had another match-winner in Alf Arrowsmith who was, according to the boot room boys, a born goal-scorer. He had been bought from Ashton United in 1960 and would become an important player in the coming season.

In the 1963/64 season the boot room philosophy began to pay dividends. Shankly had acquired many notebooks over the years and, meticulous as ever, he had written down anything he felt was useful in a simple, sensible and clear way. Paddy Crerand was once quoted in a newspaper as saying that when Jock Stein, Matt Busby and Shankly

*The first day of training, July 1963.* Left to right: *Roger Hunt, Jimmy Melia, Ian St John, Ron Yeats, Ian Callaghan, Willie Stevenson and Gerry Byrne balance the ball on their toes.*

spoke about football, a six-year-old boy could understand them.

This would be a recurring theme throughout the boot room years – simplicity coupled with planning and tried and tested methods. Everything was done with a purpose and every training session would be carefully planned. Shankly always emphasised that the simple things count. He likened it to the branches of a tree, with Bob Paisley, Joe Fagan, Reuben Bennett or Shankly himself suggesting something and then the others suggesting what could be added. It was all about trust and respect. Shankly revealed that he felt the boot room boys were like 'psychiatrists', analysing and 'brainwashing' the players. They talked about the players' strengths and weaknesses and their good habits and bad habits when playing. Shankly likened it to a 'confessional'. Meanwhile Shankly – with help from Paisley, Fagan and Bennett – had overseen continuous improvements to Melwood that transformed it into a training ground fit for champions.

Shankly was adamant that players should not be pushed too hard

*Fans queue for derby match tickets outside Anfield, September 1963.*

in pre-season training, which needed to be a gradual process. Gone were the days when youngsters like Roger Hunt and Tommy Lawrence could hardly walk after training. The initial training that brings strength at the start of the season was the big test, according to Shankly. They started five weeks and two days before the start of the season and built up gradually, which reduced the chance of injuries.

Training sessions would begin fairly gently. Reuben Bennett was the warm-up man and before they did anything strenuous he would put the players through 20–30 minutes of exercises acquired in his army days. Then, after some stretching, jogging and sprinting, the main part of the training was fast and furious five-a-side games. Invariably it would be the first team versus the reserves or else the notorious 'boot room side' of Paisley, Fagan, Bennett and Shankly. Folklore has it that the boot room team remained unbeaten for more than a decade, through a variety of underhand tactics! But these games also gave the boot room first-hand knowledge of the attributes of the squad:

who was the strongest, who was the sharpest and which players were match fit and who was struggling. It was a perfect, straightforward way to assess individual players. Shankly also introduced the 'sweat box': an invention based on a training technique used by his playing hero Tom Finney. It comprised of four numbered upright boards in the shape of a box. Two players would go inside the box and respond to instructions from the boot room boys by hitting the numbers with the balls. According to Shankly, this simple technique bred the fittest players in the game.

Whatever the secrets of the training methods, they paid off spectacularly in the 1963/64 season. Even though Liverpool lost two of their first three games, they then defeated champions Everton 2-1 at Anfield on 28 September 1963 with two goals from Callaghan. Demand for tickets for the derby match had been massive, and huge crowds queued at Anfield the week before the match to make sure they got in to see it.

*A card game on the train to London for the FA Cup fifth-round tie against Arsenal, February 1964. Liverpool won 1-0.*

'Ron Yeats said, "that we should clinch the championship on our own ground before our own fans was perfect … when we ran the lap of honour round the ground, well that was like a fairy tale ending" – but in fact the dream had just begun.'

Liverpool then went on a magnificent run that saw them take 47 points from a possible 60, including a run of seven straight wins during March and April 1964, which secured the Championship. They also went on a promising FA Cup run, reaching the sixth round, only to be beaten by Swansea 2-1 at Anfield. Once again Cup glory wasn't to be, even though within a few weeks they would prove to be the best team in the country.

When they beat nearest rivals Manchester United 3-0 on 4 April at Anfield in front of a crowd of nearly 53,000 – with a goal from Ian Callaghan and two from Alf Arrowsmith – Liverpool FC more or less wrapped up the League title in style. It was a performance of class and 'perpetual motion' according to sports journalist Norman Wynne. Liverpool played 'champagne' football and they simply outclassed Matt Busby's side. Liverpool never stopped running and never stopped shooting, and even with an 18-year-old George Best deployed for United, as a lone striker he couldn't trouble the Liverpool defence. It was reported that Liverpool's goalkeeper Tommy Lawrence was merely a spectator. The Kop chanted 'Easy, easy' and they were right.

In Shankly, Matt Busby had finally met his match. As the third goal went in to put the game beyond doubt, Matt Busby might have been thinking he should have let Shankly resign when he was trying in vain to convince the Liverpool board to spend some money! After just four seasons, with the backing of Eric Sawyer and his loyal boot room, Shankly was on the verge of achieving what seemed impossible when he arrived in December 1959. The title was nearly theirs, and

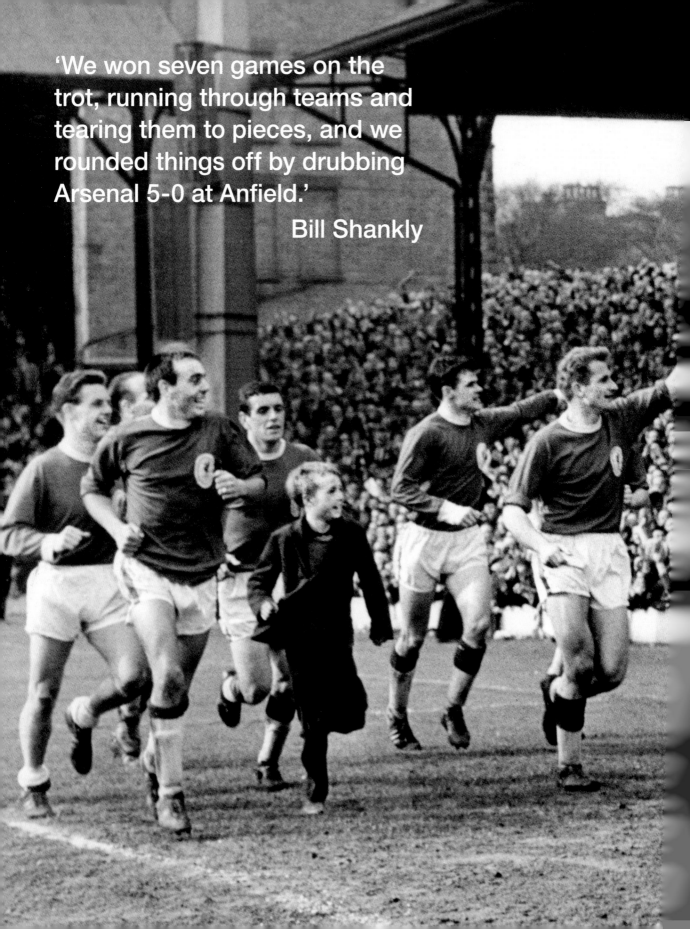

'We won seven games on the trot, running through teams and tearing them to pieces, and we rounded things off by drubbing Arsenal 5-0 at Anfield.'

Bill Shankly

*Liverpool players enjoy a bath after beating Burnley away, April 1964.*

**Previous page:** *Liverpool players on a lap of honour after beating Arsenal to win the League Championship.*

after beating Burnley 3-0 away in midweek on 14 April, Liverpool just needed to secure a win against Arsenal at Anfield on the Saturday to be crowned champions.

When Liverpool played Arsenal, the gates at Anfield were closed an hour before kick-off and the Kop had been singing for an hour before that. The BBC's *Panorama* programme had dispatched a TV crew to report on the 'extraordinary cultural phenomenon' of 28,000 Kopites singing and swaying on the packed terrace. The rise of Liverpool FC as a force in football had coincided with 'Beatlemania', with international attention focusing on the explosion of Merseybeat from the city's cellars. The Spion Kop was booming and the Kopites were becoming famous for singing many of the songs recorded by Liverpool artistes. In fact by spontaneously appropriating the pop hits of the day Liverpudlians were blazing a trail. Before the Kop adopted pop songs the only singing at football matches was the communal orchestrated singing at FA Cup Finals.

*Roger Hunt pours tea for the players after their 3-0 win at Burnley.* Left to right: *Alf Arrowsmith, Ron Yeats and Willie Stevenson.*

This was a completely different phenomenon, and the *Panorama* TV crew couldn't have chosen a better game. With the ground full and a swaying mass of humanity behind the goal, they captured the Kop singing a magnificent version of 'She Loves You', by The Beatles, and 'Anyone Who Had a Heart', a Burt Bacharach song recorded by Liverpudlian Cilla Black. Liverpool had already adopted 'You'll Never Walk Alone' earlier in the season, when Gerry and the Pacemakers had secured a No. 1 with a version of the famous Rodgers & Hammerstein song from the musical *Carousel*.

*Panorama* presenter John Morgan described the scene as the players walked onto the pitch, then the scenes on the Kop: 'The gladiators enter the arena, the field of praise, Saturday's weather perfect for an historic Scouse occasion … they don't behave like any

*St John scores the first goal against Arsenal, April 1964.*

other football crowd, especially not at one end of the Anfield ground on the Kop. The music the crowd sings is the music that Liverpool has sent echoing around the world. It used to be thought that Welsh international rugby crowds were the most musical and passionate in the world, but I've never seen anything like this Liverpool crowd. On the field here the gay and inventive ferocity they show is quite stunning. The Duke of Wellington before the Battle of Waterloo said of his own troops, "I don't know what they do to the enemy but by God they frighten me," and I'm sure some of the players in this match this afternoon must be feeling the same way.'

Geoff Strong, who was playing for Arsenal on the day but would soon become a Liverpool player, said the noise from the crowd destroyed the Gunners' morale: 'I've never heard a noise like the Kop made that afternoon in my life.' Over the next few decades many more teams would feel the noise.

*August 1964. Sitting behind the Anfield Road goal are some of the hundreds of youngsters who rushed to the ground sit after it was announced that players would pose for pictures and parade the League Championship trophy.*

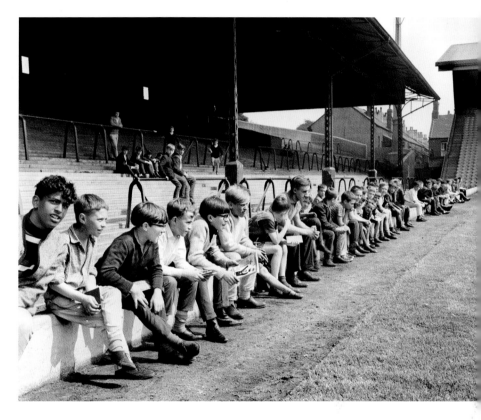

Ian St John opened the scoring for the Reds in the seventh minute, but an Arsenal penalty in the 29th minute threatened to spoil the party. Tommy Lawrence saved the penalty and was rewarded by the Kop singing 'Ee-Aye-Addio, Tommy saved a pen!' Liverpool swept to victory with one goal from Alf Arrowsmith, two from Peter Thompson and the fifth from Roger Hunt. Anfield went wild and Frank McGhee in the *Daily Mirror* reported that the Kop set this match to music and sang their team to the Championship with a wit and warmth woven into the pattern of play so closely that it became a part of the game itself.

# Chapter 5

The Holy Grail

*Excited young Liverpool fans outside the Park End, Goodison, in the Sixties.*

# The Holy Grail

After winning the League, the boot room boys set about planning how to win a trophy that Liverpool fans had long craved – the FA Cup. For 73 years the club had been trying to win the coveted trophy, without success – and Evertonians constantly reminded Liverpool fans of it. Twice Liverpool had reached the final, in 1914 and 1950; now Liverpool fans sensed that Shankly would finally bring them the FA Cup. It is hard to imagine today, but before the riches of the Champions League and the Premier League, winning the FA Cup was the ultimate domestic glory.

Liverpool's assault on Europe began with a trip to Reykjavik in Iceland in August 1964. 'Most of us didn't know where Reykjavik was,' Ron Yeats admitted. 'We flew from Manchester to London, then from London to Prestwick in Scotland, then finally caught a flight there to Iceland. When we got to Scotland we had four or five hours to kill before the flight, so Bill Shankly decided to take us to the Butlins holiday camp in Ayr. When we got there Shanks said to the

*Bill Shankly waves goodbye to his players at Manchester airport as they set off on a five-week tour of the USA in May 1964. Shankly was staying behind and travelling to Scotland to look for new talent.*

man on the gate, "We are Liverpool Football Club on our way to play a European tie in Iceland." The fella just looked at him and replied, "Oh aye, well you're on the wrong road here, mate."'

It was a happy European debut for the club in Iceland. New signing Phil Chisnall – the last player to be transferred between Manchester United and Liverpool – got his name on the score sheet as Liverpool ran out 5-0 winners in Reykjavik.

*Phil Chisnall, who made the move from Manchester United to Liverpool, scored in Liverpool's first game in Europe. When transferred he said, 'I'll have to learn more about this Liverpool sound – my brother has a guitar and I am going to practise.'*

Five days after the 'expedition' to Iceland, Liverpool opened up their defence of the League title at Anfield. The game was famous for the fact that it was the first ever to be featured in the BBC's *Match of the Day* highlights programme. As the Liverpool players ran onto the pitch towards the Kop goal Kenneth Wolstenholme introduced the footage: 'Welcome to *Match of the Day*, the first of a weekly series coming to you every Saturday on BBC2. As you can hear, we are in Beatleville for this Liverpool v Arsenal match,' he said, as 'She Loves You' blasted

*Left Ron Yeats and Bobby Moore lift the Charity Shield, which was shared after a 2-2 draw at Anfield, August 1964.*

*The boot room were so concerned about Alf Arrowsmith's knee injury that in December 1964 they bought him a bicycle to help him strengthen it.*

out from Anfield's PA system. Liverpool ended up 3-2 winners but their form in the early part of the season was disappointing; they won only two of their first eight fixtures, losing five and drawing one. Whether it was the distraction of European competition or simply the loss of two key players – St John with appendicitis and Alf Arrowsmith with a bad knee injury – the boot room decided they needed strengthening with a new recruit. Geoff Strong was that man, the inside-forward having impressed them when playing for Arsenal earlier that season. He arrived in November 1964 for £40,000 and the team's form immediately began to improve. He would be a crucial addition to the squad for the coming campaigns.

After the relative ease of their first European match, things were going to get a lot tougher in the next round as Liverpool were drawn against Anderlecht, a team that included eight Belgium internationals.

## 'That's it, that's our new kit – you look about seven feet tall!'

Shortly before the tie Shankly decided to unleash his secret weapon. After discussions with Paisley, Fagan and Bennett it was decided that they should abandon the white shorts and white socks with red trim and go for an all-red kit. They felt it would make the players look bigger and more formidable, so after training one day Ron Yeats was called into Shankly's office. At first Ron Yeats thought he might be getting a wage rise, but Shankly wanted him to try on this all-red strip. Yeats remembers that he got changed into it but then couldn't find Bill Shankly or Bob Paisley anywhere so he walked out of the players' tunnel to find them. They were standing in the middle of the pitch and as he came out Shankly shouted, 'That's it, that's our new kit – you look about seven feet tall!'

*Bill Shankly greets Anderlecht captain Jef Jurion at Speke airport.*

Shankly remembered that the kit had a huge psychological effect. 'Our game against Anderlecht at Anfield was a night of milestones. We wore the all-red strip for the first time. Christ, the players looked like giants. And we played like giants.' They swept the Belgium champions aside 3-0 with goals from St John, Hunt and Yeats. Liverpool also won the away leg 1-0 at the Heysel Stadium in Brussels with a late goal from Roger Hunt. The headlines read 'The Pride of Belgium Shattered.'

*Ron Yeats, who Shankly thought looked 'seven feet tall' in the new all-red kit.*

As 1965 approached with no chance of a title challenge, fans' attention turned to the FA Cup. They were drawn away against West Bromwich Albion and over 5,000 fans headed for the Hawthorns. Goals from Hunt and St John brought victory in a tricky fixture in which they were also able to blood youngsters like full-back Chris Lawler and inside-forward Tommy Smith. The journalist Horace Yates described the win as a 'true team triumph', explaining that Liverpool's strength didn't come from individuals but from an 'expert welding of numbers'. He observed that one of the true tests of a great side is that it is possible to introduce youngsters like Lawler and Smith without an apparent weakening of the team.

Next up for Liverpool were Stockport County, who were then bottom of the Fourth Division. Shankly was so confident of victory at Anfield that he left the boot room stalwart Bob Paisley in charge of the team and went to watch their next European opponents, Cologne.

*Shankly signs autographs after returning to Speke airport after the Anderlecht away victory.*

Stockport went one up and although Gordon Milne equalised in the 51st minute they could only draw. The crowd of over 52,000 were shocked that Stockport held on for a replay and they could have been forgiven for thinking it was the same old story in the FA Cup. Liverpool, however, had no such problems in the replay, playing in the all-red kit, and they strolled to victory with a 2-0 win, both goals coming from a lethal Roger Hunt.

*Callaghan scores for Liverpool against Bolton at Burnden Park in the fifth round of the FA Cup with only five minutes remaining.*

Liverpool had avoided a potential slip-up, but there was another banana skin coming up in the form of Second Division Bolton. By now Liverpool fans had 'cup fever' and over 20,000 of them turned up at Burnden Park to see a late goal by Ian Callaghan secure a passage to the FA Cup quarter-finals.

Liverpool fans' optimism turned to gloom when they drew bogey team Leicester in the next round. Leicester had beaten Liverpool in their last three League games and had also beaten them in the 1963 FA Cup semi-final. In seven games Liverpool had lost six times to Leicester and only won once. The game at Filbert St ended in a 0-0 draw, but Roger Hunt's winner in the replay in front of a crowd of 53,000 at Anfield got the fans believing again. The Leicester City voodoo had been broken and Liverpool were in the semi-final against Chelsea.

But before that they had another European tie to play against West German champions Cologne. In the first leg in Germany they earned a 0-0 draw, and even though Liverpool bombarded the Cologne goal

Liverpool fans celebrate at Burnden Park after Ian Callaghan scores Liverpool's winner.

*Ron Yeats re-enacts the coin toss that put them through to the semi-final of the European Cup after arriving back at Liverpool airport, 26 March 1965.*

in the second leg at Anfield, they couldn't beat the visiting goalkeeper, who was outstanding. 'Schumacher crammed a lifetime's glory into that game,' said Shankly. 'It's because of him we have to go to a replay.' Played at a neutral ground, Rotterdam's Feyenoord stadium, that replay also ended in a draw – and was steeped in controversy. After a pulsating tie that ended 2-2 after extra time, the match would be decided by the toss of a coin. This of course was before the days of penalty shootouts! Liverpool captain Ron Yeats chose 'tails' but incredibly the coin landed on its edge in the mud and the coin had to be tossed again. Soon the Liverpool players were jumping for joy, but for both sides it was a disappointing finish. Everyone agreed it was a farcical way to decide who went through to the semi-final against Inter Milan.

The FA Cup semi-final against Chelsea was played in front of nearly 68,000 people at Villa Park and Liverpool commanded proceedings from the start. Their exertions in Holland didn't seem to have affected them and they looked sharp and dominant. Just after the hour, winger Peter Thompson put Liverpool in front with a glorious left-footed strike past Chelsea keeper Peter Bonetti.

Liverpool continued to attack and then with just over ten minutes left Willie Stevenson converted a penalty after 'Chopper' Ron Harris lived up to his name and brought down Ian St John in the penalty area as he was about to shoot. Liverpool fans went wild as the final whistle went and thousands swarmed onto the pitch. Liverpool were in the final against Leeds United, Liverpool were Wembley bound, and maybe this was finally going to be their year!

*Left Liverpool club secretary Jimmy McInnes dealing with the flood of telephone calls and letters requesting tickets to the FA Cup Final, only a few days before the team's match against Leeds at Wembley.*

*Right St John is mobbed as he leaves the pitch after Liverpool reached their first Cup Final in 15 years.*

Demand for Cup Final tickets was enormous. Liverpool officials and players were inundated with requests, but they were only going to be allocated 15,000 tickets by the Football Association. Bearing in mind Liverpool had regularly been attracting crowds of over 50,000 to Anfield and everyone of a red persuasion wanted to go to the final, there were going to be a lot of disappointed fans. The club secretary and former player Jimmy McInnes had to deal with the requests daily. He was a great friend of Bill Shankly and a trusted servant of the club who had been in his post since 1955. Such were the demands during this period that McInnes often spent the night in his office on a camp bed. One evening shortly before the 1965 Cup Final, Bill Shankly entered Jimmy's office. McInnes was at his desk, surrounded by sacks of letters asking for tickets, the telephone ringing constantly, his camp bed in the corner. Shankly could see he was shattered. 'Still the most popular man at Anfield,' Shankly joked as the telephone rang out. 'No,' McInnes replied. 'Still the most unpopular man at Anfield.'

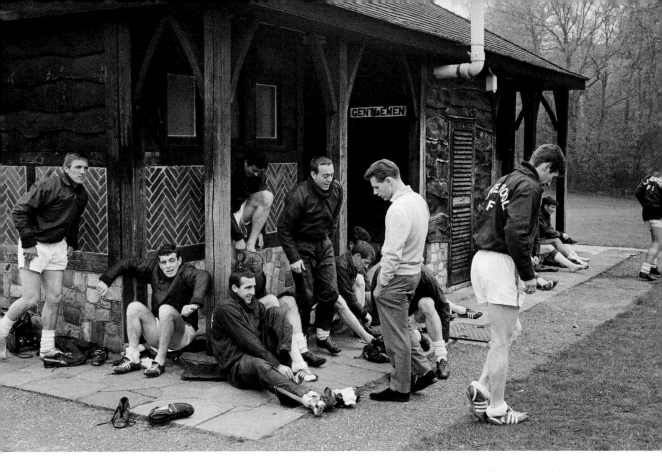

*Gordon Milne talking to his team-mates at a training session in Weybridge, Surrey, the last one before the Cup Final against Leeds – sadly for him he had failed a fitness test earlier in the week.*

Shankly announced that any spare tickets that came his way were 'going to the boys on the Kop'. Meanwhile Shankly and the boot room had their own pressing issues: injuries to Milne, St John and Callaghan. A couple of days before the final, Gordon Milne failed a fitness test, so recent signing Geoff Strong would play in his place.

It was a terrible blow for Milne, who had played an important role in the Cup run, but luckily Callaghan and St John had both been declared fit after intensive training at Melwood. The Liverpool contingent travelled to London by train midweek and spent the night before the big match watching Ken Dodd at the London Palladium.

The next morning Bill Shankly could be heard on *Desert Island Discs* choosing his favourite songs including 'My Love is Like a Red Red Rose' by Kenneth McKellar, 'Danny Boy' by Jim Reeves, 'Because You're Mine' by Mario Lanza and of course 'You'll Never Walk Alone' by Liverpool's own Gerry and the Pacemakers. That week The Beatles were No. 1 in the charts with 'Ticket to Ride' but they didn't feature in Shankly's selection.

The build-up to the game was pure theatre. Shankly walked on

Injured Gordon Milne stands in the goalmouth at Wembley Stadium the day before the FA Cup Final against Leeds United.

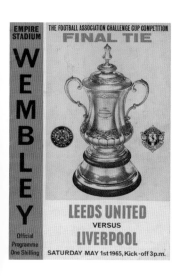

the pitch to salute the Liverpool fans who were lucky enough to get tickets, and when the teams lined up and the national anthem was played, thousands of Scousers sang 'God Save Our Gracious Team' over it. Wembley had never seen anything like it. Shankly had told the team their moment had arrived and they should go out and die for the fans. The player who epitomised that philosophy was Gerry Byrne, who suffered an injury early on in the game. He had damaged his shoulder in a collision with Bobby Collins, the captain of Leeds United. Bob Paisley, who was acting as the team's physio, felt Byrne's shoulder and immediately knew the left-back's collarbone was broken. In those days no substitutes were allowed, and Gerry Byrne decided to carry on and kept the severity of his injury to himself. The first 90 minutes were a disappointment and ended 0-0, but during extra time Liverpool's superior fitness began to show and within a few minutes they went ahead with a header by Hunt from a cross by Byrne.

Leeds soon hit back with an equaliser from Bremner, but in the second period of extra time, with both sides tiring, Callaghan crossed and St John stretched backwards to head the ball into the Leeds net

Liverpool captain Ron Yeats introduces the team to the Duke of Edinburgh before kick-off.

Gerry Byrne and Gordon Milne parade the FA Cup in front of the Kop before the European Cup semi-final against Inter Milan.

with nine minutes left. As the final whistle went Liverpool fans were ecstatic and 'Ee-Aye-Addio, We've Won the Cup' echoed around Wembley Stadium.

All the boot room's hard work, all the training, all the discussions, all the analysis and all the five-a-side games had paid off – Liverpool had finally won the FA Cup. In just over five years Shankly had achieved

*Willie Stevenson carries Ron Yeats during the lap of honour.*

what seemed the impossible dream. My own dad was a season ticket holder and was lucky enough to get a ticket for the match off Albert Shelley, but my granddad, who had lived in Anfield all his life and had supported Liverpool since their formation when he was a small boy, had gone to his nephew's wedding. When he was told the final score the 83-year-old burst into tears. He was not the only one. The messiah and the boot room boys had delivered the FA Cup – now for the European Cup.

The boot room had done their homework on Inter Milan; they knew their strengths and weaknesses. They knew that their manager Helenio Herrera, who had developed the defensive system called '*catenaccio*' (meaning 'bolt the door'), would try and keep it tight. The atmosphere was electric, with the gates shutting two hours before the match. As the crowd worked itself into a frenzy, Shankly sent Wembley hero Gerry Byrne and injured Gordon Milne out with the FA Cup. Journalists searched for superlatives and Shankly would say later, 'The noise was unbelievable, people were hysterical, it was the greatest night in the history of Anfield.'

The Italian and World champions were simply overwhelmed. In the fourth minute Roger Hunt put Liverpool ahead, but a lapse in concentration allowed the Italians to sneak an equaliser. From then on Liverpool gave Inter a footballing lesson, totally outclassing them and scoring a further two goals through Callaghan and St John. As the Kop sang 'Oh Inter one two three. Go back to Italy' to the tune of 'Santa Lucia', it seemed Liverpool were destined for European glory. When Herrera said after the match, 'We have been beaten before, but tonight we were defeated,' nobody disagreed. Shankly said it was one of the best games he had ever seen.

Celebrations were short-lived, however, as the day after the Anfield triumph against Inter, Shankly was informed that his close friend and club secretary Jimmy McInnes had killed himself. The overworked 53-year-old Scot had been found hanging from an archway in the Kop – he had given his all to the club. From the heights of euphoria,

*Left 12 May 1965. Liverpool footballers Ian St John and Ron Yeats relax on the shores of Lake Como at their base in Cernobbio, near Milan. It was the calm before the storm!*

Shankly was devastated. Whatever the reasons for McInnes's suicide it was quite clear that Liverpool as a club were not prepared for the success Shankly had brought them. The club's infrastructure was still set up for dealing with a mediocre Second Division outfit, but they were now dealing with success and the massive demands that came with it. A Liverpool official said at the time, 'He was a great guy to us. He must've been working under a terrific pressure in the last few months.'

For Shankly, sadly, there was little time to mourn. Even though traumatised by the death of his friend, he had to prepare the team for the away leg of the European Cup semi-final in Milan.

In the days before the game, the Italian press had worked the 90,000-strong crowd into a frenzy, citing supposed underhand tactics used by Liverpool at Anfield that basically amounted to Shankly sending out Gerry Byrne and Gordon Milne with the FA Cup. The hostile Italian crowd fired rockets, lit bonfires and threw smoke bombs and coins to create a poisonous, intimidating atmosphere. Liverpool players were abused and spat at, and Shankly described the proceedings as 'a war'.

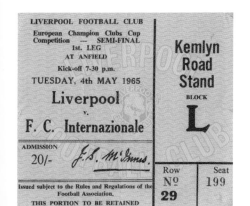

Liverpool lost the match 3-0 and their chance to become the first British team to reach the European Cup Final had gone, after a series of controversial refereeing decisions. The memory of that night would haunt the boot room boys and the players for many years to come, but it taught them the vagaries of European football. It was a bitter lesson for Liverpool Football Club but one they would learn from. Herrera admitted Liverpool were one of the finest teams in the world, and Shankly was convinced they were. Their experiences in Milan would help the club in future campaigns.

# Chapter 6

## Champions Again

*Till Death Us Do Part stars Warren Mitchell and Tony Booth supporting West Ham and Liverpool respectively during their match at Anfield in January 1967 filmed as part of the sitcom.*

# Champions Again

After the FA Cup triumph in May 1965 Liverpool fans were on top of the world, but behind the scenes all was not well. Bill Shankly was dismayed at what he thought was a derisory bonus the board of directors had offered the team and the staff. 'I've ended a 73-year wait by this club to win this trophy and this is all you think it's worth.' The Liverpool players were usually paid a 'special' bonus if gates at Anfield were over 50,000, so Shankly thought they should be paid an extra bonus for playing in front of 100,000 at Wembley. But the directors disagreed. The dispute rumbled on for most of the summer until it was finally resolved in favour of the board, and once again Shankly was left feeling that the board didn't appreciate the value of the players and the boot room. His numerous run-ins with the directors did at least produce one of his legendary quotes: 'At a football club, there's a holy trinity: the players, the manager and the supporters. Directors don't come into it. They are only there to sign the cheques.'

The boot room were convinced that Liverpool's success was

Above *Willie Stevenson, Chris Lawler and Gerry Byrne take off their football boots after completing a training session.*

based upon their fitness, and in the 1965/66 season they used just 14 players. Out of those, Alf Arrowsmith played in only five matches and youngster Bobby Graham just one. Pre-season training was the key to everything if Liverpool were to challenge for the title again, after a disappointing League campaign in 1964/65. As always everything was planned meticulously. After the summer break, when the squad came together again in July, Reuben Bennett would perform the warm-ups, and then the players would split into six groups: A, B, C, D, E and F. As Shankly later revealed in his autobiography, 'At the beginning of each season the groups would be listed on the noticeboards and the trainers would be given about a dozen foolscap pages of notes which they consulted every day.' Each group would be given a different task, which included weight training, jumping, skipping, squats, stomach exercises and sprints. After a set time they would move on to another task until they had all completed the circuit. Then the squad would be given a ball and would go through various footballing drills, ending up with small-sided games of usually five-a-side.

Bill Shankly was undoubtedly the inspiration behind many of the training methods and playing style, but he was never really a coach in the true sense of the word, as his forte was management. As for Bob Paisley, in Joe Fagan's autobiography *The Reluctant Champion* it is revealed that even though he was officially a coach, Paisley was 'more of a quiet observer day to day as well as carrying out a key role as chief physiotherapist'. Joe Fagan helped to give players treatment, but his foremost role was planning individual training methods, and leading training alongside Reuben Bennett.

Joe Fagan was also the reserve team manager and his task was to prepare his players to play 'the 'Liverpool way'. A simple style of football was drilled into each member of the squad. Pass and move, pass it to the nearest red shirt, help each out, work as a team! This simple style suited the boot room boys, as they all believed that no one player was more important than another. Joe Fagan was extremely popular with the players, and Ron Yeats said of him, 'I found Joe to be one of the most unassuming and down to earth men I was to come across in football.' The role of each member of the boot room was crucial and Ian St John thought the same: 'No football men have devoted themselves to a cause so thoroughly and self-effacingly.' St John also revealed that if disciplinarian Reuben Bennett ever heard any of the squad criticising or spreading doubts about team selections or tactics, 'he would pin him against the wall'. He was either put right or sent on his way.

As far as the players were concerned, there was no coaching hierarchy at Melwood and they remember Joe Fagan being unflinchingly loyal to Shankly and Paisley. While responsibility for training was shared between the boot room boys, one of Joe Fagan's duties was to organise and record each day's schedule. Joe's little black books were nothing more than A4 notebooks, but as Ronnie Moran testifies, they were the encyclopaedias that would define Liverpool's approach for three decades. Moran was still playing in the 1965/66 season, but when he joined the boot room a few years later he used them as a 'priceless source of reference'.

*Below All smiles at pre-season training in July 1965, but only after Shankly's dispute with the Liverpool board had rumbled on all summer over what he thought was a derisory bonus offer for winning the FA Cup.*

*Liverpool players Ian Callaghan (centre) and full-back Gerry Byrne (right) signing autographs with Bob Paisley at Manchester airport before leaving for Turin to play Juventus.*

Liverpool started the 1965/66 League campaign with an impressive 3-1 win against Leicester City at Filbert St, with two goals from Roger Hunt and one from Geoff Strong. Although they lost 1-0 to Sheffield United at home in the next game they put five past West Ham at Upton Park and hammered Everton 5-0 at Anfield at the end of September. In one of the most one-sided derby matches ever seen, Everton were completely and utterly humiliated, and the boot room put it down to Liverpool's preparation. Shankly had told his staff that he had seen Everton training from the bedroom of his house, which overlooked their training ground at Bellefield – contradicting his famous quote that 'if Everton were playing at the bottom of the garden I'd pull the curtains'. On this occasion he didn't pull the curtains, and he revealed to the boot room that Catterick had his players running

'As the Kop celebrated before the final whistle, the mood at the Anfield Road end of the ground turned ugly.'

lap after lap around Bellefield. He predicted they would be 'knackered' for the match – and it appeared he was right.

With Liverpool winning the Cup last season, their attention now turned to the Cup Winners' Cup. In the opening round of matches they had been drawn away to Juventus. The memory of the 'battle of Milan' was still fresh in their minds, so it was with some trepidation that they travelled to Turin at the end of September. But Liverpool had learned from their earlier experience in Milan, and Shankly and the boot room boys had told the team to be patient and defend. On this occasion the players were pleased with the Hungarian referee who three times turned down impassioned pleas for a penalty from Juventus players. The plan to keep a clean sheet seemed to be working until a fierce drive from Leoncini gave the Italians a one-goal advantage to take to Anfield.

For the return leg Anfield was bursting at the seams and in fine voice. A crowd of 51,000 roared Liverpool on to a 2-0 victory with a header from Lawler and a fierce shot from Strong. In his match report journalist Albert Barham praised the teamwork and understanding of a side that he said had no equal in fitness and in purpose in England. Liverpool's reputation was soaring in Europe, as Juventus were regarded as one of the finest sides around. After coming through two bruising encounters with Standard Liège and then beating Hungarian side Honvéd, in April 1966 Liverpool were drawn against Celtic in the semi-final of the European Cup Winners' Cup. Bill Shankly was going to come head to head with his great friend Jock Stein – the manager of Celtic – in an encounter dubbed the Battle of Britain. The first leg in Glasgow wasn't one for the purists, however, and Liverpool were poor by their standards as they were hustled and bustled out of their stride, going down 1-0.

Buoyed by their slender 1-0 lead, Celtic fans came down to Merseyside en masse expecting to see their heroes triumph, but Liverpool had other plans. In Glasgow they had been without Roger Hunt through injury – the second leg would be an entirely different affair. In a gripping encounter Liverpool took a 2-0 lead through a

*Anfield groundsman John Roberts clears up after the Celtic bottle party.*

Tommy Smith free-kick and a Geoff Strong header, but just before the end Bobby Lennox had a goal disallowed for offside. As the Kop celebrated before the final whistle, the mood at the Anfield Road end of the ground turned ugly, and bottles thrown by Celtic fans rained down on the Liverpool goal. Tommy Lawrence was forced to take refuge out of range of the bottles outside the penalty area and the referee wisely decided to blow the whistle without any injury time. The next day the Liverpool ground staff claimed to have collected 4,000 bottles and cans, some of which were lined up on the boundary wall. Bill Shankly famously asked Jock Stein if Celtic wanted their share of the gate receipts or just wanted the empties back (in those days bottles could be returned for money).

Liverpool were in their first European final, but before that they needed to wrap up their second League title in three years. Liverpool had topped the table since December and only needed to draw at home against Chelsea at the end of April to secure the title. Before the game Tommy Docherty's side formed a guard of honour and

Top left *Chelsea players form a guard of honour as Liverpool players run on for the last home game of the season, 30 April 1966. Lawrence leads out Byrne, Callaghan and Smith.*

Top right *Roger Hunt scores to secure the title for Liverpool, 30 April 1966.*

Right *Liverpool players parade the League Championship trophy in front of their ecstatic fans following the 2-1 victory over Chelsea. Left to right: Gerry Byrne, Peter Thompson, Willie Stevenson, Ron Yeats (holding the replica trophy), Tommy Smith, Tommy Lawrence and Chris Lawler.*

applauded the Reds onto the pitch. There was no doubt that Chelsea expected Liverpool to be crowned champions that day and they were right, as Roger Hunt scored two more goals, bringing his tally for the season to 30 League goals in 37 games.

Winning the title having used only 14 players all season backed up the boot room's belief that Liverpool were the fittest and strongest side in the land as well as the best. Tommy Docherty said after the game, 'Liverpool are a great side. Their record over the past four years

*Wags of the 1960s. Liverpool footballers and their wives attend the opening of Betsy St John's hairdressing salon in Walton.*

speaks for itself and their fans are the best fans in the world.' No one was going to argue with that.

Ever since the Kop had adopted songs in the early 1960s, they had been the envy of the football world, and up and down the country supporters began to copy them. There was something unique about the swaying mass of humanity that occupied the famous terrace. Their roar had always been loud, but when they started to adopt popular songs they went to another level. Bill Shankly especially felt he was one of them and he was extremely proud of their reputation. 'Forget The Beatles and all the rest,' he once said. 'This is the real Liverpool sound. It's real singing, and it's what the Kop is all about.' Liverpool supporters adopted Shankly as an honorary Scouser and he even said, 'Although I'm a Scot I'm proud to be called a Scouser.'

The worldwide popularity of The Beatles and other groups had made Liverpool one of the world's most fashionable cities, and in films and television everyone seemed to want a Liverpool connection.

*Peter Thompson poses with his fiancée Barbara Ponting, surrounded by his Liverpool team-mates at the opening of his new garage near Anfield.*

Sitcoms such as *The Liver Birds* were in production and *Till Death Us Do Part*, although set in East London, included a Liverpudlian character played by Cherie Blair's father Tony Booth. Even Hollywood wanted an association, and Yul Brynner appeared in a crime thriller based in Liverpool and London called *The File of the Golden Goose*.

The Liverpool players were also in high demand and many were opening their own businesses – even during the season. I wonder what Bill Shankly thought of that! Players' wages were a fraction of what they are today, so they needed to think about investing for their future. Peter

*Members of the England squad relax at their Liverpool hotel before a friendly. Left to right: Peter Thompson, Bobby Charlton, Gordon Milne and Roger Hunt. Thompson and Milne were unlucky and didn't make the final World Cup squad.*

Thompson opened a garage near the ground and Ian St John's wife Betsy opened a hairdressing salon in the Walton area of Liverpool.

Football-mad Liverpool fans were anticipating the next big Cup Final and they didn't have long to wait. Shortly after winning their seventh Championship, Liverpool were in the European Cup Winners' Cup Final against Borussia Dortmund at Hampden Park in Glasgow. On a wet Thursday evening in Scotland, Liverpool's European dreams were once again shattered. Liverpool never reached the heights of their previous form that season but at least they did shake the Germans in the second half after Held had scored for Borussia

'It looked like there was only going to be one winner, but Liverpool could not break the German defence.'

against the run of play in the 61st minute. Liverpool then threw everything they had at Borussia and Roger Hunt's equaliser in the 68th minute sparked a massive pitch invasion from the Liverpool fans who seemed to make up most of the 41,000 crowd. It looked like there was only going to be one winner, but Liverpool could not break the German defence. In extra time Liverpool continued to attack and appeared to be the fitter, stronger side, but in the 107th minute

*Liverpool and Everton captains Ron Yeats and Brian Labone, a Scot and an Englishman, were unlikely team-mates during the World Cup – as the area representatives for World Cup souvenirs.*

Borussia scored the winner after a Tommy Lawrence clearance found midfielder Libuda, who lobbed the ball back over the keeper. The ball hit the post and then rebounded off Ron Yeats into the net. It was a freak goal, but it meant Borussia became the first German team to lift a European trophy.

Liverpool players and staff were absolutely devastated; they had deserved to win but they had been denied victory by a lucky goal. They had proven they were the greatest team in England but

once again had just come up short in Europe. Bill Shankly was still convinced they were the best team in Europe, but the record books would show them as beaten semi-finalists and beaten finalists in 1965 and 1966. Now attention turned to the 1966 World Cup, which was to be held in England.

Following Liverpool's success in the mid 1960s, Roger Hunt, Gordon Milne, Ian Callaghan, Peter Thompson, Tommy Smith, Gerry Byrne and Chris Lawler were all called up to the initial squad of 40 for England, but only Hunt, Callaghan and Byrne were selected for the final squad.

After England's World Cup triumph in the summer, the first competitive match on Merseyside was the Charity Shield. Liverpool and Everton, League and FA Cup winners respectively, met at Goodison Park in August 1966. It was a historic occasion as England heroes Roger Hunt of Liverpool and Ray Wilson of Everton paraded the Jules Rimet trophy around the pitch. Then Ron Yeats came out with the League trophy and Brian Labone came out with the FA Cup. Merseyside appeared to be the centre of the footballing universe. However, proud Scot Bill Shankly wasn't overly impressed by the World Cup success. Roger Hunt remembers how the manager greeted him when, after a couple of days off, he reported back for pre-season training with Liverpool. 'All he said to me was "Well done, son, but we've got more important things to do now!"'

*Hunt and Wilson parade the World Cup around the ground before the game.*

# Chapter 7

## The Rebuild

*Willie Stevenson, Ian St John and Ron Yeats wear their woolly hats during a training session on 27 January 1967.*

# The Rebuild

In 1966 Liverpool seemed to be on the cusp of greatness. The returning World Cup winners in the squad may have been greeted by a shrug of the shoulders, but in reality the boot room boys were genuinely proud of their international achievements. But now it was back to the business that mattered to them, winning more trophies for Liverpool, especially the European Cup they felt they had been cheated out of in 1965. Everton had just bought World Cup winner Alan Ball from Blackpool and were able to get their revenge for the hammering the previous season by beating Liverpool 3-1 at Goodison. Alan Ball scored two of those goals which left Liverpool in 16th position after three games. But Liverpool's form did recover, and they were eighth in the League by the time they played Petrolul Ploieşti in the first round of the European Cup.

The Romanian champions were no match for Liverpool, and it was eventful in more ways than one: it was my first European match – a birthday treat from my dad. I was too young to remember much about the game, but I remember the sights and sounds of the Kop and the strange-sounding name of the opposition. I was hooked!

Liverpool continued to climb up the table, and by the time they faced Ajax of Holland in the second round of the European Cup in December they were in third place, just two points off the top. Little was known of Ajax at the time and when Roger Hunt heard the draw, he said the players were delighted as they thought Ajax would be one of the weaker teams. On a foggy night in Amsterdam, Liverpool's dream would become a nightmare. Bill Shankly wrote in his autobiography: 'Ajax had the makings of a team then, but they were not yet the great team that they later became. We played them first in Amsterdam, but the match should never have started. The fog was terrible.' When Liverpool went two goals down, Shankly actually walked onto the fog-bound pitch while the game was in progress and said to Stevenson and Strong, who were trying to attack: 'Christ, this is only the first game. There's another bloody game at Liverpool, so we don't go and give away any more goals. Let's get beat 2-0. We are not going too bad. Take it easy.' He later revealed: 'I walked on to the pitch, talked to the players, and walked off again – and the referee never saw me!'

The boot room were in shock. Europe had been a learning curve over the years, but they were all convinced they were preparing to take Europe by storm and this was their year. Their eventual 5-1 defeat in Holland sent shock waves through Europe, but Shankly wasn't a defeatist and he tried to convince everyone who'd listen that Liverpool could overturn the four-goal deficit. He blamed the fog in Amsterdam, he blamed the referee, he blamed the pitch – he blamed everything. He convinced both the players and the fans that Ajax weren't that good, and a couple of early goals would be the start of a historic comeback. The Kop was so packed for the second leg that many spectators spilled onto the pitch. As steam rose from the packed Kop, the hoped-for comeback didn't materialise, even though Liverpool were unlucky, hitting the woodwork twice during early frenzied attacks. Just after the break Ajax showed their undoubted class when a young Johan Cruyff put the visitors ahead on 49 minutes.

*A youngster is helped from the crowd during the home game against Ajax. It was a tradition for people in distress, especially youngsters, to be passed over the heads of Kopites. It happened to me in a game against Manchester United in the early 1970s when i came off a barrier I was sitting on and couldn't get back to it.*

Roger Hunt pulled one back for Liverpool, but then Ajax went ahead again with another goal by Cruyff in the 70th minute. Hunt helped restore some pride with his 88th-minute equaliser, but the dream was over. Liverpool had drawn 2-2 on the night but lost 7-3 on aggregate. Many football analysts look back at those matches and say it was the start of the Dutch revolution – the beginning of manager Rinus Michels's 'Total Football' that would dominate the international game in the 1970s. For the Ajax players it was like a fairy-tale, and the Dutch maestro Johan Cruyff often called it his favourite game.

When reporters suggested that Shankly and the boot room had maybe underestimated the Dutch side they were furious, but in their heart of hearts they knew the team needed strengthening. The

*Roger Hunt scores Liverpool's second goal in the 2-2 draw with Ajax – who won 7-3 on aggregate.*

*Above right This is what it meant to beat Liverpool 7-3 on aggregate. Jubilation for Ajax supporters and players at the final whistle.*

players weren't getting any younger and after lengthy discussions in their traditional Sunday morning get-together in the boot room, Bob Paisley, Reuben Bennett, Bill Shankly and Joe Fagan all agreed the team needed fresh legs. Time was moving on and some of the key players were probably past their peak. Ron Yeats would soon be 30 and Ian St John, Roger Hunt and Gerry Byrne were all in their late twenties. Something needed to be done, and at the start of 1967 it was decided that new blood was needed to maintain Liverpool's position as a force in English football, never mind Europe. Having watched him for several months, the boot room identified Emlyn Hughes from Blackpool as their main target, and in February 1967 they bought him for £65,000.

The boot room had also identified Preston North End star Howard Kendall as a target and Liverpool put in a bid for the promising youngster. Preston North End had strong links with Liverpool through Bill Shankly, and the fact that they had sold Gordon Milne and Peter Thompson to them. However, Preston didn't want to be viewed as a feeder club for Liverpool FC, so their board rejected the bid outright. They feared that their fans would be in uproar, having already seen their best players sold to Liverpool. Bill Shankly was convinced that if

*Emlyn Hughes holds his football boots which he took away from the ground after signing for Liverpool.*

Liverpool went back with an improved offer they would get their man, but the saga dragged on, even after Kendall put in a transfer request. Kendall stated in his autobiography *Love and Marriage* that he even went to stay with Peter Thompson for a weekend at his digs – he expected to be transferred to Liverpool, so he wanted to get to know the city.

Behind the scenes, with no publicity, Everton were also showing interest in buying Kendall. As the transfer deadline loomed, Kendall found out from Jimmy Milne, the Preston manager (and Gordon's dad!), that the club had sold him to Everton for £85,000. Liverpool FC had been outbid, and Bill Shankly was furious with the board for not securing the deal. He actually sent a letter of resignation, but it was not accepted, and the letter remained unopened in Liverpool secretary Peter Robinson's desk for many years. Shankly believed the club hadn't tried hard enough to get Kendall. Maybe they had been put off by Preston's asking fee for a 19-year-old, or maybe once again they were doubting his judgement – even after all the success he had brought them and all the eulogies they had given him when Liverpool won the League the year before.

There was only one thing for it – if he still wasn't trusted to spend

*Bill Shankly watches new signing Hughes during a training session with the reserves at Melwood.*

*Geoff Twentyman was recruited by Bill Shankly to become chief scout in 1967. He would become the unsung hero of the boot room.*

big money after all he had done for the club, he needed someone to scout young potential stars. Shankly and the boot room needed someone they could trust implicitly, a football man who knew the club and shared the same philosophy and principles as them. Shankly turned to Geoff Twentyman, who had played for him at Carlisle and also knew the rest of the boot room as he had played for the Reds 170 times between 1953 and 1959. In *Secret Diary of a Liverpool Scout* by Simon Hughes, Ronnie Moran explained why they turned to Twentyman in their hour of need, 'Shanks wanted people around him who wanted to be winners, and he also wanted people who loved their jobs and would work hard.' Twentyman was such a man, and he was arguably one of Shankly's greatest signings – he would go on to become one of the unsung heroes of the boot room.

Even though Liverpool had dominated English football since the 1963/64 season it had become obvious that instead of continuing their reign they had lost their cutting edge. The Liverpool fans

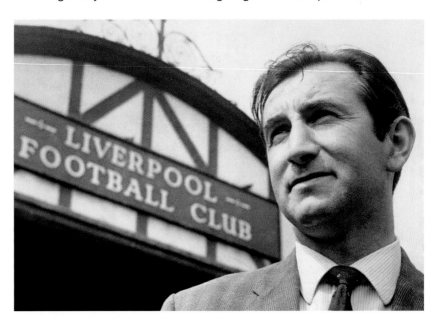

stayed loyal, though, as many could remember the doldrums of the Second Division and Shankly was looked upon as a miracle worker. If he had done it once, surely he had the answers to rejuvenate an ageing squad. Twentyman's brief was to scout young players

Liverpool could afford, and the boot room would transform them into Liverpool players. Joe Fagan, who oversaw the reserves, would then nurture these protégés until they were ready for the first team. Fagan had reared Lawrence, Lawler and Smith in the early 1960s; now Twentyman would scout the new crop of youngsters with a 'northern soul' and Fagan would teach them the 'Liverpool way'. In the past Shankly had used contacts all over the country to recommend players, but now he had someone he had total confidence in, and Twentyman was about to build up his own network of scouts he could trust.

In 1968 Tom Saunders also joined the boot room. He was appointed the youth development officer on a part-time basis, becoming full-time in 1970, dealing with schools in Merseyside and the North West. A former school teacher, Saunders managed Liverpool and England schoolboys during the 1960s and recommended many local prospects to the boot room. Shankly trusted his judgement, so asked him to join the set-up. Saunders hadn't played the game like the rest of the boot room, but as his role evolved and his reputation grew, he himself became a key member of the inner sanctum. Saunders was in fact the only member of the boot room who held a coaching

*Manager Tom Saunders with the Liverpool schoolboys team, who had won the English League Division One Schools Trophy in 1966/67.*

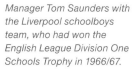

*Liverpool FC, August 1967.*

certificate. Bill Shankly was not a huge fan of coaching certificates, as he showed shortly after the World Cup when he was obliged to lead a Liverpool delegation to the FA coaching centre at Lilleshall. Uninspired by having to spend so much time listening to 'theory', he cut his stay short by declaring to Bob Paisley, 'Come on, Bob, we've heard enough.' But he obviously saw qualities in Tom Saunders that could serve Liverpool Football Club well.

After the disappointments of the 1966/67 season, the boot room realised that their biggest problem was not enough goals. When Liverpool won the League in 1965/66 they had scored 79 goals with Roger Hunt netting 29. The following season they were down to 64 goals with Hunt scoring only 14. St John's goal tally was 9 in the League. To solve their goal-scoring problem Liverpool brought in Tony Hateley from Chelsea for £96,000. He started off well, scoring a hat-trick in his second home game against Newcastle, but he would only make 56 appearances. He linked up well with Roger Hunt, but he wasn't the ball-playing centre-forward Liverpool were looking for, so in 1968 Liverpool spent £100,000 on teenager Alun Evans, a blond-

*The seaside retreat in Blackpool was supposed to be a secret – but young fans watch through the hotel window as Tony Hateley and Emlyn Hughes play snooker. April 1968.*

*Bill Shankly listens to the FA Cup draw with some of his players over lunch at Anfield. Left to right: Emlyn Hughes, Ian St John, Alun Evans, Bill Shankly, Tommy Smith, Ron Yeats and Geoff Strong.*

haired forward with an eye for goal.

One of the main reasons the boot room had decided to sign Alun Evans was because he had given Ron Yeats such a hard time and scored when he had played for Wolves at Anfield the previous season. They saw he had skill, was quick and courageous and could find the net. Liverpool scouts were often seen at Wolves games, and it was soon decided that he had all the essentials to play for Liverpool. At the time, it was a massive fee for a youngster who had only played 20

First Division matches. Evans, nicknamed the 'Kidderminster Beatle' due to his long hair, started off well. Wearing the No. 9 shirt on his debut at Anfield, he scored in a 4-0 win over Leicester City. His next match was against his old club Wolves at Molineux and resulted in a 6-0 hammering for the home side. Evans scored twice and many thought Liverpool had solved their goal-scoring problems. Shankly warned Evans after the match, 'Don't say anything, son. Don't be going to newspapermen … and saying Wolves made a mistake in selling you … because it can blow back in your face.' Shankly wanted to keep the youngster's feet on the ground, and for a while everything seemed to be going well for him. But disaster struck in a Wolverhampton nightclub when he was injured by a bottle in the face. After that Evans had terrible luck, and Shankly was convinced that this incident had been deeply damaging to him. In his first season he only

*Below Alun Evans in action for Liverpool against Leicester City, 21 September 1968.*

*Above right Two young fans show interest in Alun Evans's damaged eye, September 1970.*

found the back of the net seven times in 33 League games and in the 1969/70 season – which was curtailed by injury – he scored only three times in 19 League games. The boot room knew they had to look elsewhere to make Liverpool a force again.

Shankly had tried to blend youngsters with the older members of

*Scorer Barry Endean is congratulated as Watford FC defeat Liverpool in the fifth round of the FA Cup.*

the 1960s team but it all came crashing down on 21 February 1970 in the FA Cup quarter-final against Watford at Vicarage Road, when a Barry Endean goal put them out of the FA Cup. It was the last straw for Shankly and the boot room – a watershed moment. It wasn't just the defeat; it was the manner of the capitulation that convinced them all that enough was enough. Only a select few survived the cull that followed.

No one said it would be easy, but the break-up of the 1960s team after the Watford debacle would show the importance of the boot room. The defeat had made them all realise that introducing youngsters like Ray Clemence, Bobby Graham, Brian Hall, Peter Wall, Ian Ross, Steve Peplow and John McLaughin from Joe Fagan's successful Central League reserve team was not the answer. A clear-out had to happen. Many supporters thought Shankly had been too loyal to his beloved Sixties side, but now he knew he had to act. In his autobiography he wrote: 'After Watford I knew I had to do my job and change my team. I had a duty to perform for myself, my family,

Liverpool Football club and the supporters, who had been used to success … it had to be done, and if I didn't do it, I was shirking my obligations.' Gerry Byrne soon went because of injury, but Shankly now had to leave out the spine of his team that had brought most of the mid-Sixties success, and it was not without heartache. Lawrence, Yeats, St John and Hunt would soon be on their way, and the boot room often had to smooth things over. Roger Hunt remembers the writing was on the wall when Shankly approached him before a match and asked him how he thought he was playing. Roger replied that he thought he was doing well, to which Shankly remarked, 'Well, the

*Roger Hunt with the Kop in the background.*

## 'I ranted and raved. They were trying to calm me down but it was futile work.'

directors don't think so.' Hunt came back with 'When have you ever taken any notice of what the directors think, boss?' To which Shankly replied, 'You're right, son. Get your shirt on, you're playing!'

It was Joe Fagan in particular who had to use all his man management skills to manage the fall-out between Shankly and unhappy Sixties legends. Although he loved that team, Shankly didn't handle the break-up very well. Before an away game at Newcastle, St John had only found out from the legendary Newcastle player-turned-reporter Jackie Milburn that he wasn't playing. Milburn had been handed the team sheet and told the Saint he wasn't in the line-up. Shankly had dropped St John without saying a word to him. St John was livid and stormed back to the dressing room. In his autobiography St John remembered: 'Shankly was nowhere to be seen … I ranted and raved. Bob Paisley and Reuben Bennett were trying to calm me down but it was futile work.' When Bob Paisley told St John to warm up during the match, St John refused, saying he would only warm up if Shankly came down from the stands to ask him personally. He didn't. St John remembers going home on the team bus in complete silence.

On the Monday after the match, St John went straight into to Shankly's office at Anfield to confront him. 'Why didn't you tell me I wasn't playing?' he asked. 'After all these years didn't you think I deserved better than hearing it on the steps of another football ground?' The confrontation ended in a full-blown row with yelling and cursing, and St John was put with the reserves later that day at training, and it was left to Paisley and Fagan to pick up the pieces of the fall-out. Paisley could certainly empathise with him; he had been left out of the 1950 FA Cup Final after scoring in the semi-final. He knew the pain St John was going through and was able to remind him of all the great times they had shared and witnessed. Joe Fagan's compassion and understanding also helped to ensure that players left with the dignity their years of service had warranted. The Watford game was more or less the end of St John's time at Anfield; he played a few games for the reserves, but only two more first-team games. Hunt had already been sold to Bolton Wanderers after his contract expired in December 1969. Tommy Lawrence played just one other

game; only Ron Yeats played on and made another 16 appearances
the following season before slowly giving way to Larry Lloyd, who had
been signed on the recommendation of Twentyman.

The Swinging Sixties were over, the Beatles were about to 'officially'
break up, Neil Armstrong had walked on the moon, regular colour
television broadcasts had begun on BBC, and Liverpool v West Ham
was chosen as the first *Match of the Day* in colour. The Ford car
factory in Halewood, which was taking over from the docks as one
of the major employers in the city, had suffered its first dispute and
industrial unrest was simmering. Nearly 140,000 people had left the
city, most of them moving to new estates on the outskirts such as
Kirkby, Cantril Farm, Skelmersdale, Netherley and Speke. As the new
decade began, Simon and Garfunkel had just released their album
*Bridge over Troubled Water* to critical acclaim and Geoff Twentyman
was travelling up and down the country looking for new talent to
restore the fortunes of Liverpool FC. They ended the 1969/70 season
in fifth spot – 15 points behind the champions Everton. Liverpool
needed someone to work another 'miracle' if they were to get back to
where they belonged.

*With Liverpool directors, officials, players and wives, Bill Shankly and presenter David Coleman (left) watch* Match of the Day *being screened in colour for the very first time. It featured their match against West Ham United, November 1969.*

# Chapter 8

The Second Coming

*John Toshack arrives at Lime Street*
*Station with his wife Susan and is greeted*
*by Bill Shankly, 11 November 1970.*

# The Second Coming

The first signing of the new decade was hardly high profile but it would turn out to be very astute. In May 1970, 22-year-old Steve Heighway, the flying winger, was bought from non-League Skelmesdale United after being spotted by Geoff Twentyman. The Dublin native's unorthodox style of play on the left wing would prove a great asset to Shankly's new-look team. He was a graduate like Brian Hall, who would also play an important part in Shankly's second great team. The pair were affectionately called 'Big Bamber' and 'Little Bamber': a reference to *University Challenge* host Bamber Gascoigne and Brian Hall's lack of height.

Later that year, Twentyman persuaded Bill Shankly to have a look at the prolific goal-scorer John Toshack as he had European experience with Cardiff City. In his scouting diary, in the entry for 6 November 1970, Twentyman had written, 'Very good in the air, does a job we want.' Shankly agreed, and within a week Toshack was a Liverpool player, signed for £110,000. Toshack was a wonderful header of the ball and with Heighway on the wing things were finally looking up.

Toshack admits that he found it hard at the start as he could feel the weight of expectation on his shoulders. He was under pressure to be an immediate success at a high level. When he arrived in Liverpool, the first thing Shankly said to him was 'You're coming out of Sunday school and going into church.' Toshack knew exactly what he meant.

Geoff Twentyman was aware that while he was scouring the country for new talent, Liverpool couldn't go out and sign too many £100,000-plus players. He concentrated on finding another hidden gem like Steve Heighway in the lower divisions, but fate would also play a part. When Andy Beattie – Shankly's old team-mate at Preston and managerial boss at Huddersfield – tipped Liverpool off about a youngster playing for Scunthorpe, Shankly asked Twentyman to check him out. Twentyman liked what he saw, and on his recommendation Paisley, Fagan and Shankly went to watch Kevin Keegan in a second FA Cup replay between Scunthorpe and Tranmere Rovers at Goodison Park. The selection of the neutral location for the second replay was down to the toss of a coin, and if Scunthorpe had won the toss it would have been Hillsborough rather than the convenient Goodison Park – and the boot room might never have seen the young Kevin Keegan. On the evidence of that one game they all agreed he had the attributes to be a Liverpool player and they signed him for £33,000 in May 1971. Liverpool had been lucky with tossed coins.

Thanks to all the transformation and rebuilding, in the 1970/71 season Liverpool finished a creditable fifth and also managed to get to the final of the FA Cup. In an exciting semi-final at Old Trafford they had beaten Everton 2-1, Brian Hall and Alun Evans scoring after Liverpool had gone 1-0 down to their rivals.

In the final, the new-look Liverpool side were to face Bertie Mee's Arsenal, who had just won the League and were sitting 14 points ahead of Liverpool. Shankly was fielding a young side and even commented, 'We have got to Wembley with a team of boys.' With all their youngsters, Liverpool put in a determined performance and it was 0-0 at full time. When Heighway put Liverpool ahead in the 92nd minute it looked like they could lift the Cup in the energy-sapping sunshine. However, goals from Eddie Kelly and Charlie George won

*Kevin Keegan signs for Liverpool from Scunthorpe United in May 1971, watched by Peter Robinson, the Liverpool secretary, Ron Ashman, the Scunthorpe manager, and Bill Shankly.*

*Steve Heighway closes in on the Everton goal in the FA Cup semi-final at Old Trafford, 27 March 1971.*

the Cup for Arsenal in the dying moments. Shankly thought Liverpool had thrown it away. 'We had the game won when Heighway scored his goal,' he said afterwards. 'It was all over. I would have laid odds of four to one against Arsenal scoring. In a position such as that I thought nobody could beat us.' The only consolation for Liverpool was that they were a young, transitional team.

*With the score 0-0 after 90 minutes at Wembley, Bill Shankly and the boot room boys encourage their players before extra time.*

*Thousands of people lined the streets of Liverpool to welcome their heroes back from London and were addressed by Bill Shankly from the steps of St George's Hall.*

The team's homecoming the next day has gone down in Liverpool FC folklore. Shankly returned home with his defeated players to a remarkable turnout. It was as if they had won the Cup and I will never forget it. I was there as a wide-eyed schoolboy and even though I was inconsolable at the loss, Shankly's speech on the steps of St George's Hall made us all feel like glory was just around the corner. After thanking the fans for their wonderful support he said, 'Since I came here to Liverpool and to Anfield I've drummed into our players time and again that they are privileged to play for you and if they didn't believe me, they believe me now.' He promised to return to Wembley to lift the Cup and we all believed him.

In the close season there was a reshuffle in the boot room set-up. Due to Joe Fagan's success as the reserve team manager, he was officially recognised by promotion to the first team as a trainer. Bob Paisley was made assistant manager and Ronnie Moran was put in charge of the reserves. Moran had only just retired from playing,

having wound down his career in the reserves, but was still totally committed to the Liverpool cause. As first team coach Joe Fagan continued to take the training sessions, but now he was given more of a hands-on role with first team players. Most clubs had clearly defined roles for each coach but at Liverpool everyone mucked in and everyone supported each other.

The 1971 Cup Final had been a major disappointment, as Larry Lloyd remembered: 'We were all in tears and at a moment like that you feel as if you are never going to recover.' But recover they did, and it was Kevin Keegan who was the catalyst for the second great Shankly team. It became obvious in pre-season training that Keegan wouldn't be getting groomed in the reserves like everyone else. Keegan played just three reserve team games; the week before the season began, he excelled in one of the traditional first team v reserves games. Usually these games were stalemates because the reserves gave it everything while the first team were just trying to avoid injury. In one match while

*Bill Shankly, aged 57, practises his football skills at the training ground, June 1971.*

he was playing for the first team, Keegan gave the experienced Ian Ross the run-around, so Shankly decided to start him in the first game of the season. Supporters didn't know much about Keegan and when he turned up at Anfield for his Liverpool debut even one of the stewards refused to believe he was a Liverpool player. 'I will never forget my debut,' recalled Keegan. 'There were fifty thousand inside Anfield and thirteen minutes in I scored, in front of the Kop as well. It doesn't get any better than that … unbelievable. Like a fairy-tale.'

Kevin Keegan ignited the new team and in the 1971/72 season the Toshack/Keegan partnership blossomed. Liverpool went very close to winning the League. Liverpool needed to beat Arsenal at Highbury in the last game of the season to pip Brian Clough's Derby County to the title. Liverpool bombarded the Arsenal goal, and with two minutes left on the clock Keegan crossed to Toshack for a tap-in to make it 1-0. Liverpool thought they had won the title until the referee Roger Kirkpatrick blew for offside. Shankly called it a diabolical decision. 'That man deprived us of the First Division Championship,' he raged after the final whistle. 'It is a heartbreaking thing to happen to my young lads after their magnificent challenge.' Shankly said Liverpool's performance was perfection and they had fought like tigers, but one thing was certain: Liverpool were on the up, and it wouldn't be long before they were lifting silverware again …

The mood in the camp was upbeat at pre-season training in 1972. The Liverpool squad had been bolstered by the addition of skilful midfielder Peter Cormack for £110,000 from Nottingham Forest, equalling the club record set by the signing of John Toshack. Shankly called Cormack the last piece of the jigsaw. Brian Hall, who had graduated from the reserves under the watchful eye of the boot room to become an important part of the 1972/73 team, remembers: 'There was always great optimism in the camp and at the start of the 72/73 season it was no different. That was very much the nature of Bill Shankly. He inspired confidence in the lads. If he told us once, he told us a thousand times that we were the greatest.'

After playing a few reserve team games, Peter Cormack was called up into the side with Brian Hall making way. For the first time in several

*Bill Shankly addresses
the squad at Melwood.*

years the Liverpool side had more or less picked itself: Clemence, Lawler, Lindsay, Smith, Lloyd, Hughes, Keegan, Cormack, Heighway, Toshack and Callaghan. Local youngsters who had been groomed in the reserves like Phil Thompson and Phil Boersma were knocking on the door of the first team, as well as the ever-dependable Brian Hall. The emphasis was on teamwork and Kevin Keegan maintains that the 1970s team were 'one of the greatest of all passing sides'. Liverpool swept to their record eighth Championship, three points ahead of Arsenal and seven above Leeds.

In the early Seventies I had started going to the matches on my own, and I was at the home game against Leicester when Liverpool clinched the title. I have never witnessed anything like it before or since. I had queued from midday to get into Anfield and get my spec' on a barrier near the middle of the Kop. I always tried to sit on the barriers as I was too young (and short!) to see. The atmosphere was incredible and even though it was a drab 0-0 encounter against

Leicester, we were there to acclaim Shankly's second great team.

The lap of honour was chaos as thousands ran onto the pitch to celebrate their heroes. The communion between Shankly and the fans was incredible, with Shankly's name resounding from the Kop to the tune of 'Amazing Grace'. The feeling was mutual – Shankly adored the fans as well. On this day Bill Shankly was well and truly immortalised.

Shankly said that winning this title had given him more pleasure than the previous two in the mid-Sixties, simply because he'd had to rebuild the side. In the 1968/69 season, Liverpool had come close to winning a trophy by coming second, and they came third in 1970/71, but they hadn't won anything for seven years. Fortunately, in those days before social media and 24-hour sports coverage, the fans appeared to be willing to let the boot room get on with their jobs and

Right *Bill Shankly celebrates with the League Championship trophy as his side become champions following their goalless draw with Leicester City at Anfield, 28 April 1973.*

rebuild a dynasty that would dominate domestically and in Europe for years to come.

After achieving domestic glory, Liverpool had less than two weeks to prepare for the UEFA Cup Final first leg against Borussia Mönchengladbach at Anfield on 9 May. Since their disappointment in the 1966 European Cup Winners' Cup Final, Liverpool had continued to be involved in Europe, but had never reached a final again. This was an opportunity for Shankly's new breed to achieve what the 1960s team had never been able to do and lift a coveted European trophy. Once again the weather would have a massive influence on the game. Surprisingly in the first leg Brian Hall had been picked in front of John Toshack to face the Germans at Anfield. However, after only 27 minutes the match was abandoned as a torrential downpour had made the pitch unplayable. The following evening, Toshack was back in the side as the boot room had spotted a weakness in the German defence in the air. Kevin Keegan, described by journalist Harry Miller in the *Daily Mirror* match report as 'a greyhound in football boots', teamed up with Toshack to tear the German defence apart in a frantic 12 minutes midway through the first half in which Keegan found the net twice. Keegan also missed a penalty that would have given him a

*John Toshack soars between two defenders during the first leg of the UEFA Cup Final against Borussia Mönchengladbach at Anfield.*

deserved hat-trick, but a second-half Keegan corner found the head of Larry Lloyd and Liverpool had a three-goal advantage going into the second leg.

In Germany, the classy Borussia team went 2-0 up in the first half but they seemed to run out of steam in the second, and Liverpool held on to lift their first European trophy. It had taken Liverpool eight years and a number of bitter disappointments to lift European silverware, and after the match Shankly declared: 'Next season we're in Europe again, playing in the number one competition, the European Cup – now for the big one.' Even though publicly Shankly said the title was Liverpool Football Club's bread and butter, he really wanted to win the European Cup. He had been haunted by the nightmare of Milan in 1965 and he wanted to put things right. He was building a team capable of European glory.

Reuben Bennett, Bob Paisley, Bill Shankly and Ronnie Moran on the bench at the UEFA Cup Final second leg in May 1973.

As Liverpool win their first European trophy, on 23 May 1973, fans invade the pitch and carry Kevin Keegan aloft.

December 1973. Kevin Keegan
and Steve Heighway eat their
lunch by candlelight during the
Three-Day Week.

There were incredible scenes when the Liverpool team came home.
They arrived in the early hours of the morning and Speke airport was
full of fans. Shankly said that seeing them made it all worthwhile, but
it was nothing compared to the welcome they got later in the day
when the open-top bus travelled from Anfield to the Picton Library on
William Brown Street in the city centre after a ten-mile motorcade.

Liverpool FC may have been in the ascendancy, but in the
autumn of 1973, after a series of anti-inflationary measures by the
Conservative government (elected in 1970 under Ted Heath), an
international oil crisis emerged. Sparked by a surprise Arab attack on
Israel and a work-to-rule by the miners, a three-day working week was
imposed to conserve energy. Sales of candles reached an all-time
high as the blackouts took hold. Football matches under floodlights
were banned, and power cuts were the norm. In December 1973 the
government announced a set of emergency measures including a
50mph speed limit on all roads; a reduction in street lighting; and a
heating limit of 63°F in all office and commercial premises, which
included Melwood and Anfield. Only essential services were exempt
from the measures, but thankfully in March 1974 the restrictions were

Left to right: *Phil Boersma, Liverpool-born boxer John Conteh (who had just retained his European light heavyweight title) and Tommy Smith with the UEFA Cup wave to the crowds during the homecoming celebrations.*

Following page: *William Brown Street is packed with Liverpool fans welcoming their heroes home following their victory in the UEFA Cup Final.*

lifted and thing slowly turned back to normality.

Even though Liverpool had won a domestic and European double the previous season, football was evolving, and the style of football that Liverpool had experienced in December 1966 against Ajax had been widely adopted on the continent. Liverpool got off to a good start in the European Cup, beating minnows Jeunesse Esch of Luxembourg 3-1 in the first round, but the boot room's dream of a successful run in Europe came crashing down in the second round when they met Red Star Belgrade. The Yugoslav outfit produced some magnificent football, playing from the back and outclassing Liverpool in both legs to win 4-2 on aggregate.

The morning after the home leg, Bill Shankly was joined by Bob Paisley, Joe Fagan, Reuben Bennett and Ronnie Moran in the boot room for a post-mortem. This would turn out to be one of the most important boot room meetings ever held. Everyone articulated their thoughts and the consensus was that Liverpool had to adapt their style of play if they were to succeed in Europe. They had to be more patient and build from the back. 'The top Europeans showed us how to break out of defence efficiently,' Bob Paisley later recalled. 'The

pace of their movement was dictated by their first pass. We had to learn how to be patient like that and think about the next two or three moves when we had the ball.'

*Outside Wembley Stadium before the FA Cup Final against Newcastle, 4 May 1974.*

In deciding to adopt a continental style of football by slowing the game down, the boot room were ahead of the game in England. On the muddy pitches of the First Division it was a courageous decision, but it was also an enlightened move that would serve them well in the years to come. The new style of play meant the old-fashioned centre-half stopper was a thing of the past, and the ball-playing Phil Thompson replaced Larry Lloyd. After their disappointing European Cup exit, Liverpool concentrated on trying to make up ground on Leeds United. Leeds had made a magnificent start to the 1973/74 season to try and take the title, but a combination of injuries, suspensions and indifferent form left them wanting. It was during this season that Roy Evans made his last two appearances for the first team before being persuaded to go into coaching. Liverpool's form improved as the season went on, but they couldn't catch Leeds United, who finished five points clear of second-placed Liverpool.

They never looked like missing out in the FA Cup Final. True to his words on the steps of St George's Hall in 1971, Shankly's Red Army had returned to Wembley to face Newcastle after beating Doncaster Rovers, Carlisle United, Ipswich Town, Bristol City and Leicester City on the way. Liverpool's new continental style of play was perfectly suited to the Wembley pitch. The pre-match build-up had been dominated by Malcolm Macdonald and his promise to demolish the Liverpool defence, which meant there was no need for a team talk. Shankly simply pinned up an article Macdonald had written, with the headline 'We Are Going to Win the Cup', on the notice board of the team hotel. 'There you are, boys,' he said. 'That's what they are going to do to us.' It was one of the most one-sided finals anyone can remember as Liverpool strolled to a 3-0 victory, giving an exhibition of continental style football. The future looked bright – nobody could imagine what was in store!

*Two Liverpool fans kiss Bill Shankly's feet after the 3-0 victory over Newcastle.*

# Chapter 9
The Reluctant Hero – Bob Paisley

*Manager Bob Paisley at Anfield on 10 April 1978.*

# The Reluctant Hero
# – Bob Paisley

Just after midday on Friday, 12 July 1974 the unthinkable happened. Bill Shankly announced his retirement. The boot room were as shocked as everyone, having had no inkling of the bombshell. It was a JFK moment for Liverpool fans, and many refused to believe it, as did most of the players and staff. Television crews wandered the streets and captured the bewildered reaction of the people of Liverpool. When Tony Wilson of *Granada Reports* gleefully informed Liverpool supporters in the city centre that Shankly was retiring, hardly anyone believed him. One Evertonian simply responded, 'Thank Christ for that.'

Shankly had been at Liverpool just short of 15 years and had totally transformed the fortunes of the club. Even though he had made his mind up, he later said, 'Coming to my decision was like walking to the electric chair.' We will probably never know the real reasons behind his decision, but Shankly felt confident that he had left the club in a healthy state with a brilliant team and a great boot room to carry on the dynasty. With his retirement in mind he had made Bob Paisley

*Liverpool manager Bill Shankly greets young fans outside the directors' office at Anfield on the day he resigned as manager of the club, 12 July 1974.*

assistant manager, confident that he, along with the rest of the boot room, could continue the 'bastion of invincibility' seamlessly. Like everyone else, even Bob Paisley wasn't convinced by the news at first. 'Every year, virtually, he'd say he was going to pack in. You didn't take him seriously. When he finally did I was lost for words, shocked. It was the day I got back from holiday and it was like a bomb being dropped.' It was no less shocking for T.V. Williams, who had met Shankly outside Huddersfield's ground in 1959 to offer him the Liverpool job. At the press conference the chairman wept openly – it was the end of an era!

A fortnight after Shankly's retirement, Bob Paisley was announced as the new manager. The board of directors had decided that Paisley was ideally suited to carry on the good work Shankly had started. Club secretary Peter Robinson was quoted as saying, 'The fact that Bob would have such a strong staff behind him … was a contributory factor in the high level of confidence we placed in Bob.' Paisley and almost everyone else in the inner sanctum had pleaded with Shankly to change his decision, but he had made his mind up and that was it. However, Shankly still thought he had something to offer and at

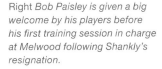

Left *Bob Paisley stands on the Kop after taking over as Liverpool manager following the resignation of Bill Shankly, 26 July 1974.*

Right *Bob Paisley is given a big welcome by his players before his first training session in charge at Melwood following Shankly's resignation.*

the start of the 1974/75 season he turned up at Melwood to offer his advice. It wasn't a successful move. The players still called him 'boss', so something had to give, and Paisley had no choice but to have a quiet word with him. Having got the go-ahead from the board, he asked Shankly to stay away so he could get on with the job. It could have been handled better, but as a club Liverpool had seen the demise of Manchester United after Matt Busby (who was also still viewed as 'the boss' by many of the club's players and staff) retired and Liverpool didn't want to make the same mistakes as United.

Bob Paisley may have only reluctantly agreed to take on the job, but he knew he had a loyal boot room to support him. Joe Fagan was the first team trainer, Ronnie Moran oversaw the reserves and, at the age of 25, Roy Evans had been brought into the set-up after only making 11 appearances for the Reds as a player. The boot room obviously saw some coaching potential in Evans as they persuaded him to hang up his boots and join them.

Bob Paisley had always been by Bill Shankly's side during his reign, giving him advice and eventually being given the title assistant manager, but Paisley was more at home in the boot room environment. Now he had the keys to the manager's office, he didn't really want things to change – after all, why change a winning formula? Few managers in the game had a better knowledge than Paisley, and with Geoff Twentyman as chief scout, the club were hoping it would be business as usual. Paisley decided to carry on as Shankly did, so he still spent most of his time in the boot room with Joe Fagan, Ronnie Moran, Roy Evans, Reuben Bennett, Tom Saunders and Geoff Twentyman. But in the reshuffle, Joe Fagan effectively became Paisley's assistant, and Roy Evans was put in charge of the reserves. During this period John Bennison also joined the boot room, to help Tom Saunders with youth development, so even though Shankly the great motivator had gone, the engine room was still operational. During the Shankly years the boot room had been very influential, but now it was going to become the focal point of Liverpool Football Club.

Bob Paisley didn't find it easy when he first took over. Not only did he have to deal with the problems brought by Shankly's apparent

*Bill Shankly chats to youngsters outside his home shortly after resigning as manager of Liverpool.*

reluctance to let go, he had to deal with issues involving the players. Paisley would later recall that 'the difficult part of the job was in handling the personal problems. I believe I had the respect of the players when I was in charge of coaching, but I had no experience of handling the players in other ways. Bill had always done that; then in 1974 I was manager and I found that job no bed of roses. I found it tough.' Paisley regarded his first season in charge as a bit of a failure as they had only finished runners-up, two points behind Dave Mackay's Derby County.

However, Paisley had been making some shrewd signings under the guidance of Geoff Twentyman. Phil Neal was bought from Northampton Town for £66,000 in October 1974, and Kirkby-born Terry McDermott soon followed him. McDermott had impressed the boot room with his performance against Liverpool for Newcastle in the FA Cup Final. Paisley was building on the foundations Shankly had laid. But McDermott had to spend nearly two seasons in the reserves and started to doubt whether he made the right decision to leave

*Bob Paisley welcomes Phil Neal to Anfield, 9 October 1974. Neal was signed for £66,000 from Northampton Town.*

Newcastle and regular first team football. This is when the boot room team came into their own. 'It was getting me down big time,' McDermott reflected. 'Luckily I had the likes of Roy Evans, who was the reserve team manager, and Geoff Twentyman to get me through it.' At Anfield patience was a virtue.

There was no doubt about Bob Paisley's second season in charge. In 1975/76 Paisley led Liverpool to a League and UEFA Cup double, as Shankly had done a few seasons before. Two other players emerged that season who would become crowd favourites. Joey Jones was signed from Wrexham in July 1975 for £110,000, and David Fairclough would come through the reserves. Jones was popular because of his total commitment to the cause, his ferocious tackling and his clenched fist salute; and 'super-sub' Fairclough for his slalom-style runs with the ball and his late goals as a substitute.

As Paisley was busy strengthening his squad, Bill Shankly was busy presenting a weekend show on Radio City, a local commercial radio station. His guests included politicians, celebrities and of course people from the world of football.

On the final Saturday of the season, QPR beat Leeds to go one point ahead of Liverpool, who had a game in hand away to Wolverhampton Wanderers. To make things even more precarious for Liverpool, the title decider was in between the two legs of the UEFA Cup Final against Bruges. Liverpool had beaten Hibernian, Real Sociedad, Śląsk Wrocław, Dynamo Dresden and Barcelona to reach the final.

The first leg of the UEFA Cup Final was held at Anfield on 28 April 1976. The game got off to a sensational start, with Bruges taking a two-goal lead inside the first quarter of an hour, and they kept that lead until half-time. During the interval, shrewd tactician Paisley decided to replace John Toshack with Jimmy Case, who had become a first team squad member that season, and the move produced the desired effect. Ray Kennedy scored with a tremendous left-foot shot, and in a five-minute spell Liverpool were in front after a goal from Case and a penalty by Keegan. Liverpool would be taking a 3-2 lead to the second leg, but before that they had the small matter of winning the League.

David Fairclough finds time for a kickabout with some of the local Cantril Farm youngsters, April 1976.

*David Fairclough poses at Liverpool's new souvenir shop.*

Tens of thousands made their way to Wolverhampton to try and see Liverpool beat Wolves and lift the title. I was one of them, and the atmosphere was more like a home game, as Liverpudlians seemed to be everywhere. The stakes were high, as a Liverpool victory would see Wolves relegated. The Reds needed to win, as QPR had a superior goal difference. Steve Kindon put the home side in front in the 13th minute and in spite of incessant attacks Liverpool couldn't find an equaliser. We all feared the worst. Then, with less than 15 minutes left, Kevin Keegan got the breakthrough we had all been waiting for, and in the 85th minute John Toshack put Liverpool ahead. There was pandemonium as thousands swarmed onto the pitch through sheer joy and relief. At one point I thought the referee might abandon the match as thousands were still on the touchline behind the goal when play continued. Then in the 89th minute Ray Kennedy put it beyond all reasonable doubt by smashing a left-footed shot into the top corner – and mayhem ensued. Liverpool had won the League again, but

*Bob Paisley reading messages of congratulation in his office at Anfield, May 1976.*

also, more importantly, Liverpool fans and Kopites in particular had finally taken Paisley to their hearts. Keegan said after the match, 'This Championship is for the boss Bob Paisley. He deserves it – he just gets on with the job quietly and effectively.'

Winning the UEFA Cup in Bruges a fortnight later was the icing on the cake. Taking a fragile 3-2 lead to the second leg, Liverpool drew 1-1, with Kevin Keegan scoring, to lift the cup. Paisley was quick to say he was just carrying on the work that Bill Shankly had started, but he was also keen to praise the members of the boot room. 'We have a great family spirit at Liverpool built on a happy camaraderie which is my responsibility to encourage and maintain. In this I have been helped enormously by the staff, the men who have worked so closely with me, Joe Fagan, Ronnie Moran, Roy Evans, Tom Saunders, John Bennison, Reuben Bennett and Geoff Twentyman.'

*Following Liverpool's semi-final replay victory over Merseyside rivals Everton at Maine Road, Joey Jones is mobbed by fans who have spilled onto the pitch.*

Little did the boot room know, but this was just the beginning of the glory years. The following season Liverpool would be after the big one – the European Cup.

In 1976/77 Liverpool won the League again and also contested two finals. They qualified for the FA Cup Final against fierce rivals Manchester United by beating Everton at Maine Road in the semi-final, and after a historic comeback at home against St Étienne that is still regarded as one of the great European nights at Anfield, they beat FC Zürich in the semis to book themselves a place in the European Cup Final in Rome.

Liverpool were in line for a historic treble: something that had never been achieved before in this country. I personally had to choose between going to Wembley to see the mighty Reds play Manchester United and travelling to Rome to see us take on Borussia

Mönchengladbach – I couldn't afford both. In the end I chose the Wembley final, and in hindsight it was the wrong one!

Liverpool were favourites to win but they met a spirited United side. United took the lead early in the second half, then Jimmy Case equalised for Liverpool, and it briefly looked like there was only going to be one winner, until a deflection from a Lou Macari shot beat Clemence in goal. Liverpool threw everything at United but they just couldn't get the equaliser, and United ended the treble dream.

As fans we were all devastated, but destiny was calling. The day before the European Cup Final thousands turned up at Speke airport to wave the team off. Many fans had travelled straight from Wembley to Rome, and thousands more had gone from Lime Street on the 'special' trains, which became the stuff of legend as they ran out of water en route!

On 25 May 1977, in the Stadio Olimpico in Rome, Liverpool produced a magnificent display of football that manager Bob Paisley described as 'the best performance in the history of the club'. Right from the start Liverpool dominated the game and with the backing of over 25,000 travelling supporters they dominated both on and off the field. The first Liverpool goal was from McDermott, but Simonsen equalised for Borussia. Then a brilliantly headed goal by

*Liverpool fans on the balcony at Speke airport as their idols board their plane, bound for Rome, to contest their first ever European Cup Final, 24 May 1977.*

Tommy Smith came from a corner, and Phil Neal sealed victory with a penalty, after Keegan had been brought down by Berti Vogts. In the *Liverpool Echo*, Michael Charters wrote: 'Liverpool are the masters of Europe – the masters of how to play European football with style and efficiency, class combined with effort, individual brilliance with superb teamwork.' It was simply a glorious night and the culmination of 13 years of endeavour in Europe. Paisley had achieved something no other English manager had achieved, but he couldn't have done it without the foundations Shankly built or the words of wisdom from Joe Fagan, Ronnie Moran, Reuben Bennett, Roy Evans, Tom Saunders, John Bennison and Geoff Twentyman. Bob Paisley acknowledged this when he said, 'Bill built the house; I just put the roof on!'

*Kevin Keegan is brought down by Berti Vogts to give Liverpool a penalty in the 82nd minute. Phil Neal scored from the spot to put the game beyond doubt.*

*Jubilant Liverpool players on a lap of honour at the Stadio Olimpico in Rome.*

*Bob Paisley described the boot room's Sunday morning meetings as 'just like popping down to the local'.*

Liverpool were on top of the world, but with the euphoria came a setback. Despite helping lift the European Cup, Keegan left for pastures new, making a £500,000 move to Hamburg SV – a record signing at the time. His departure left a huge gap in Liverpool's line-up as he had been the leading scorer in the 1976/77 season. Fans were

'Liverpool were on top of the world, but with the euphoria came a setback.'

*New signing Kenny Dalglish with youngsters on the pitch at Anfield after his transfer from Celtic.*

worried Paisley had also attempted to strengthen the defence by signing Alan Hansen – a gifted centre-half – from Partick Thistle for £100,000 on the recommendation of Geoff Twentyman. While a lot of scouts thought Hansen was a bit too slow, or too relaxed on the ball, Twentyman reckoned his style of play would be perfect for Liverpool, playing the ball out from the back. Once again Twentyman had spotted something other scouts had missed.

Domestically Liverpool were being challenged by newly promoted Nottingham Forest, managed by Brian Clough. He had built an impressive side, with a former Red, Larry Lloyd, at the heart of his defence. In the 1977/78 season, Forest won the League and finished seven points ahead of Liverpool. They also beat Liverpool 1-0 in the

Kevin Keegan and his successor Kenny Dalglish have an informal chat in the Holiday Inn, Liverpool, December 1977, before they face each other in the Super Cup fixture at Anfield between Liverpool and Hamburg. One regret Bob Paisley had was that Keegan and Dalglish never played in the same Liverpool line-up.

*New signing Alan Hansen poses on the Kop following his transfer from Partick Thistle, May 1977.*

League Cup Final replay at Old Trafford after a 0-0 draw at Wembley. Over the next few years, an intense rivalry developed between Liverpool and Forest as they battled each other for domestic and European domination. Brian Clough had a lot of respect for Liverpool FC and their staff, and would visit the boot room after matches, as was the tradition. 'Some of the best ideas came from the Boot Room,' he later wrote. Ronnie Moran remembers him coming in and just sitting there like a schoolboy taking everything in.

In Europe, Liverpool were dominant again and retained the European Cup with a 1-0 win over Bruges in the final at Wembley in May 1978. The only goal came from a brilliant chip by Dalglish, after new signing and fellow Scot Graeme Souness had set him up in the 65th minute.

*Bob Paisley, flanked by Ronnie Moran and Joe Fagan, during a game against Nottingham Forest in September 1979.*

Paisley went on to win the League four out of the next five seasons and lift his third European Cup in 1981, with a 1-0 win over the mighty Real Madrid in Paris. These were the real glory days of the boot room, and Paisley had achieved success beyond the club's wildest dreams – Liverpool ruled Europe and had become, in Shankly's words, 'a bastion of invincibility'. But while the fortunes of Liverpool FC were on the up, the same could not be said for the city. Soon after the triumph in Paris, Liverpool erupted into flames as social unrest spread throughout the inner cities of the UK. In July 1981, Toxteth – an area of Liverpool with a diverse community – erupted as a result of high unemployment, mistrust of the police and social deprivation in the economic crisis. The riots, which lasted for nine days, were so severe that for the first time in England, the police resorted to using CS gas. The city of Liverpool was in shock.

*Liverpool fans at Anfield Junior Boys School ahead of their side's European Cup Final match against Bruges at Wembley, 10 May 1978.*

Later that year came news that devastated Liverpool FC fans. On 29 September 1981 Bill Shankly died – 'the Messiah' had proved to be mortal. The architect of Liverpool's success, the adopted Scouser, the man of the people, the raconteur and wit was no more, but his spirit would live on through the fans and the boot room boys.

*Manager and boot room staff celebrating their title success following victory over Tottenham Hotspur at Anfield, 15 May 1982. Left to right: Ronnie Moran, Roy Evans, Bob Paisley, Tom Saunders, John Bennison and Joe Fagan.*

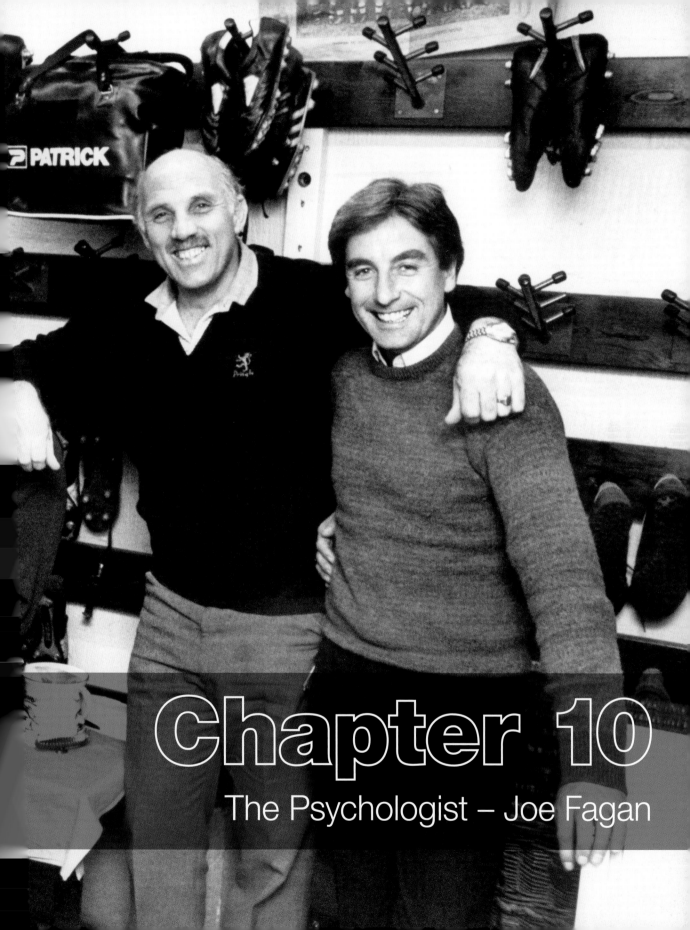

# Chapter 10

The Psychologist – Joe Fagan

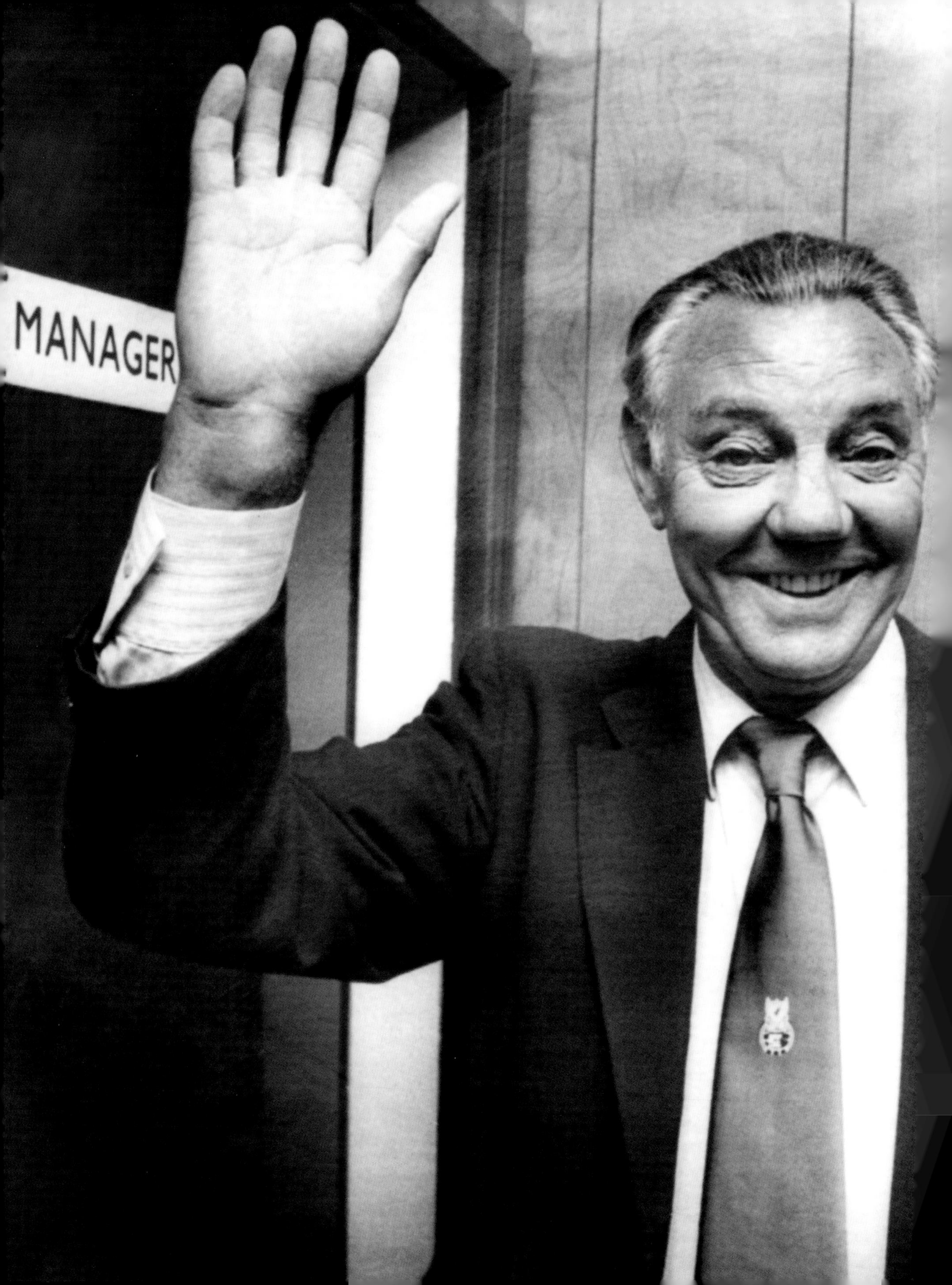
MANAGER

*From boot room boy to manager: Joe Fagan.*

# The Psychologist – Joe Fagan

Regarded by many as the heart and soul of the boot room, Joe Fagan's time came in the summer of 1983 when Bob Paisley called it a day. At the start of the 1982/83 season, Paisley had indicated that he would be abdicating. He had given 44 years of loyal service to Liverpool Football Club, having signed in 1939 just before the outbreak of the Second World War, and now it was time for someone else. Joe Fagan, like Paisley before him, didn't really want to be in the public eye, but he knew that for the sake of the club he had to carry on the boot room dynasty. The Paisley years had lasted nine seasons, bringing six League titles, three European Cups, a UEFA Cup and three League Cups. It was an unbelievable haul and it was going to be a hard act to follow. During his reign Paisley had also been manager of the year six times, but, just as Shankly did, he acknowledged it had been a team effort and that the boot room partnership was crucial.

John Smith, who had taken over as club chairman in 1973, often emphasised the word 'continuity'. The Liverpool board had no doubt

*Bob Paisley congratulates Joe Fagan on his appointment as manager.*

that Joe Fagan would provide it. When Paisley announced in August 1982 that it would be his last season, there was no speculation about who would succeed him. Everyone just presumed it would be the next in the boot room line of succession. Joe Fagan wasn't that enthusiastic, though, and later recalled: 'When Bob decide to retire, it frightened me that they may ask me to take over. I said years ago that I'd never take on a manager's job, that coaching was my game. But things do change, don't they?' Roy Evans thought that Joe decided to take the job just to keep the other members of the boot room in a job. Roy Evans said Joe was like a father figure to him, with his no-nonsense style. 'He was straightforward when he was in charge of the reserves and I was a player. If you were doing well you would get a pat on the back and if you weren't he would tell you straight. I had great admiration for Joe – all the boot room characters had different aspects. Shankly thought he was Chairman Mao, Bob couldn't talk in many ways, he mumbled instructions, but people knew what he meant, but Joe was the glue between them all.'

Alan Hansen said that when Bob Paisley announced his retirement all the players wanted Joe to become the manager, and Graeme Souness remembers that the transfer of power was 'as smooth as you'd expect'. The players obviously loved Joe, but sometimes that can be a problem when it comes to discipline. It worked out, though: if Joe's role was 'good cop', then Ronnie Moran and Reuben Bennett could be the 'bad cops'.

*A rare photo of Joe Fagan on the Liverpool bench, with Ronnie Moran, Bob Paisley (the then-manager) and Roy Evans.*

When the announcement of Joe Fagan's appointment hit the newspapers, the *Liverpool Echo* ran the headline: 'Bootroom boys still rule OK'. In the *Daily Mirror* the headline was 'I'm my own man and I'll do the job my way'.

Generally the news was well received, and Chris James of the *Daily Mirror* reported that Fagan's appointment was greeted with cheers in the dressing room. Phil Neal said, 'Joe is very popular with the lads; he doesn't beat about the bush.' Bob Paisley also gave his blessing, saying, 'I'm delighted it is staying in the family; there will be no break-up. Joe is a seasoned campaigner and he's well enough experienced to know he's got to get on with the job. I don't expect any drop in standards at Anfield – that's how much I respect him. You may have found me mean and thirsty in my search for trophies, but the bad news is the man who is taking my place is hungrier than me.'

Liverpool Football Club had learned from the outcry after Shankly's retirement, and Paisley remained involved with the club as a part-time director. And of course Joe Fagan knew he could rely on his boot room companions. The down-to-earth Scouser was now in control of one of the most successful clubs in Europe, but the only thing that would change for him was that the players would now call him 'boss'. The boot room was always Joe's home and that stayed the same even when he took over as manager. On his first day in the job, before he went to the manager's office, he popped into the boot room to have a chat with Roy Evans, Ronnie Moran, John Bennison and Tom Saunders – it was business as usual.

Fagan's appointment as manager did mean a slight reshuffle in the boot room, however: after nine years in charge of the reserves, Roy Evans was joining the first team set-up. The man Joe Fagan chose to continue the work of Roy Evans with the reserves was Chris Lawler. Lawler had been a member of Joe Fagan's reserves as a youngster before he broke into the first team in 1963. He knew all about the Liverpool way, having played 549 times for the club. He was honest, trustworthy and loyal: the perfect qualities to become a member of the inner circle, and for the first time in its history the boot room members were all born and bred in Liverpool.

Liverpool may have won the League and Milk Cup in Paisley's last season in charge, but the boot room, the directors, the fans and journalists knew the squad needed some fresh legs. John Keith, writing in the *Daily Express*, described the job of keeping Liverpool at the top as 'the most daunting in English soccer'. Joe Fagan was confident that Geoff Twentyman and Tom Saunders would find the right talent. Shankly and Paisley had always identified the type of player they wanted, then it was up to Twentyman and Saunders to find the perfect fit. On the recommendation of Twentyman, Fagan's

first signing in July 1983 was the talented ball-playing centre-half Gary Gillespie from Coventry for £325,000. After the Gillespie deal, Fagan wrote in his diary: 'Looking through the pro staff we have numbers (27) but not quality. Maybe there are thirteen players who are pretty good but after that we could do with a good player in midfield and up front. The temptation is to go out and buy now, but that could be fatal to the rest of the season if we signed the wrong ones.' An injury to Ian Rush forced Fagan into the transfer market to bolster his attack before the start of the season. A deal to buy Michael Robinson from Brighton & Hove Albion for £200,000 was quickly concluded.

Fagan's first competitive game in charge was against rivals Manchester United at Wembley in the Charity Shield in August 1983. Just before the game started, two of the greatest post-war managers, Bob Paisley and Matt Busby, circled the pitch aboard a Land Rover, hands clasped aloft. Relations between the two sets of fans might not have been harmonious, but the clubs were doing their best to calm things down on the terraces. Liverpool lost the match 2-0 but Fagan and the fans on the whole weren't too concerned, as Liverpool had played some good football, and Fagan described it after the game as 'an inevitable hiccup'.

Liverpool's opening League game against Wolves at Molineux was a disappointing 1-1 draw, and again Fagan was philosophical, saying. 'The first game of the season is always one of the hardest. There isn't quite the sharpness there yet that I'll be expecting later on.' He also commented in a club magazine on his new surroundings sitting in the stands. 'It was a strange feeling sitting up in the stands next to my chairman, rather than on the bench. I think I was the only person who

The 1984 League Cup Final between Liverpool and Everton, 25 March 1984. Managers Howard Kendall and Joe Fagan lead their teams onto the pitch.

had returned to the directors' box when Ian Rush scored 30 seconds after half-time. It is the best place for me, though. There is so much shouting going on down on the bench that they can't hear me anyway! Anyway, it's nice to get off the mark. I'm really enjoying the job. I don't know why, but I am!'

Liverpool suffered a goal drought in the first part of the season, scoring only eight in their first nine games, but the floodgates opened at the end of October when they hammered Luton Town 6-0 at Anfield with Rush scoring five. The Reds then went on a tremendous run and

'The Reds then went on a tremendous run and challengers Manchester United just couldn't close the gap.'

challengers Manchester United just couldn't close the gap. Liverpool had secured their seventh title in nine years and their third in a row. Ian Rush had broken goal-scoring records, finding the net 47 times in all competitions. Speaking to Peter Keeling of the *Liverpool Echo* at the time, Geoff Twentyman recalled how he snapped up the young Ian Rush from Chester City in 1980. 'I watched him six times and finally in an away game at Rotherham I decided that despite his youth we had to strike quickly. A lot of other clubs were holding back waiting for further proof; and don't forget Liverpool took some criticism at first when people said £300,000 was too much for a teenager.'

At the beginning of 1984, Liverpool group Frankie Goes to Hollywood had reached the top of the charts, after the BBC banned their single 'Relax' due to its controversial lyrics and artwork. In March 1984 The Beatles were given the freedom of the City of Liverpool, 20 years after they had left the city and 14 years after they had split up. The rebuilt Cavern Club on Mathew Street was about to be reopened by ex-player Tommy Smith, and Liverpool and Everton had made it to the first all-Merseyside League Cup Final.

The Milk Cup Final was held at Wembley on 25 March 1984 and was a disappointing 0-0 draw, but it was notable for the unity of both sets of fans. As a city, Liverpool was suffering from mass unemployment and political turmoil as a result of monetarist economic policies introduced by Margaret Thatcher's Conservative government. One of her election pledges had been to tackle inflation, which was standing at over 20 per cent when she came to power in 1979. To achieve this, the government raised interest rates sharply and brought in tough public spending curbs, but the measures caused a recession and mass unemployment, with areas like Liverpool particularly hard hit.

Liverpool had elected a Labour council in 1983 with election pledges to oppose Thatcher's policies, and tens of thousands of fans were wearing either red or blue stickers at the Milk Cup Final with the message 'I Support The Labour Council.' Before, during and after the match, the 100,000 crowd at Wembley sang 'Merseyside Merseyside Merseyside' – the two sets of fans had never been more united.

*Bringing home the European Cup, May 1984.*

It was an act of defiance and a unique symbol of unity in football in the face of economic hardship. In the replay at Maine Road the following Wednesday, Graeme Souness scored the only goal for Liverpool to retain the trophy for the fourth successive year. After the match, Joe Fagan was quick to praise the players and Bob Paisley, saying 'My first thought is for the players and the coaching staff … never forget it was Bob Paisley's era that brought the players here. To be honest I felt a bit embarrassed when they said they wanted to win something for me. Our club has gone on for so many years that winning trophies has become a tradition and I wouldn't like to break that.' On a wet morning after the replay, Joe Fagan wrote in his diary: 'What a lovely day whether it's pissing down or not! We won the Cup!'

It wouldn't be Joe's last trophy in his first season at the helm. After securing the title with a goalless draw at Meadow Lane against Notts County (with Joe Fagan famously sweeping the dressing room afterwards), Liverpool had 'the big one' to think about again. It would be their first European Cup Final since 1981. After two disappointing campaigns in 1981/82 and 82/83, Liverpool were back where the boot room and the fans thought they belonged. After beating BK Odense, Athletic Bilbao, Benfica and Dinamo Bucharest, they were to meet Roma on their home ground, the Stadio Olimpico. This was where Bob Paisley's 1977 team had lifted the trophy, and it had special memories for Liverpool fans. The Roma team had several of the Italian 1982 World Cup winners in their ranks, as well as Brazilians Falcão and Cerezo.

This would be my third European Cup Final in seven years. I went with 50 well-travelled Reds to Ladispoli – a seaside resort 25 miles outside Rome which had seen better days – and went to Rome by coach on the day of the match. Everywhere you went in the city banners proclaimed 'Campioni Roma', as if Roma had won already: it was obvious they thought Liverpool FC were turning up to be their sacrificial lambs. The atmosphere in the ground was frenzied as the teams walked onto the pitch. There was a primeval roar and then massive flags were passed over the heads of the Roma supporters as explosions and smoke bombs added to the electric atmosphere. Tom

Another glorious night in Rome. Liverpool manager Joe Fagan is flanked by Chris Lawler and Roy Evans *(left)* and Ronnie Moran *(right)*, 30 May 1984.

Joe Fagan did his own Italian job on Roma.

Saunders had been to watch Roma at their home ground and had reported on their formidable record at home.

Against all the odds Liverpool kept Roma quiet as Souness dominated Falcão in midfield, Phil Neal put Liverpool ahead after 14 minutes, then Roberto Pruzzo equalised on the stroke of half time. It finished 1-1 after extra time. In the penalty shootout, which has become the stuff of legend, Liverpool goalkeeper Bruce Grobbelaar pretended his nerves had gone by wobbling his legs as Roma players took their penalty kicks. Joe Fagan had told Grobbelaar to try and put them off – and it worked. When Alan Kennedy scored his penalty that was it – Liverpool were European champions once again and Joe Fagan had won a famous treble in his first season. Joe immediately embraced the boot room boys Ronnie Moran, Roy Evans, Tom

*Crowds of Liverpool fans gathered on the Cenotaph outside St George's Hall, waiting to welcome their heroes.*

*All smiles as Joe Fagan and his Liverpool players leave for Brussels for the 1985 European Cup Final against Juventus.*

Saunders and Chris Lawler. 'We were always a tight-knit group and Joe made sure it stayed that way,' says Evans. 'He involved the staff in everything he did. We won together and we lost together.' People who had doubted Fagan's ability to continue the dynasty were silenced, and Joe Fagan had joined the legends of Anfield.

In the 1984/85 season, a resurgent Everton under Howard Kendall did the double over Liverpool, beating them by a single goal both at Anfield and Goodison. Liverpool reached the FA Cup semi-final but went out to Manchester United after a replay, and with Everton storming to a 13-point lead in the League, the only chance of silverware was the European Cup. Liverpool had reached their fifth final in eight years. It should have been a showpiece of European football, but sadly 29 May 1985 will always be remembered for the deaths of 39 football fans at the decrepit Heysel stadium.

Joe Fagan had already informed the club of his intention to step down a few months before the end of the season, and he was hoping

Above centre *Training at the Heysel stadium before the 1985 European Cup Final.* Left to right: *Bruce Grobbelaar, Roy Evans, Kenny Dalglish and Mark Lawrenson.*

Above right *Liverpool and Juventus fans in the Grand Place Brussels on the day of the match.*

by the end of it to have led Liverpool to their fifth European Cup. All parties had agreed to keep the news of Joe's departure secret until after the final, but the story leaked out on the day of the match. It even came as news to the rest of the boot room, so closely had the secret been guarded. But if the headlines on the day of the match were all about Joe Fagan leaving, the headlines the following day were unimaginable. I witnessed the tragedy unfold during a surreal night of chaos, confusion and violence; sporadic fighting in the neutral stands led to a charge by Liverpool fans, which caused a breezeblock wall to collapse in the dilapidated stadium. Rocket flares also added to the panic as people attempted to flee the trouble. Before the match started I remember team captain Phil Neal, then Joe Fagan, making announcements over the public address system. Joe's son Stephen believes that having to walk across the running track and address the crowd 'was one of the most difficult things Dad ever had to do. It must have been a horrendous ordeal and watching him have to do that

*The day after the Heysel stadium disaster, Joe Fagan speaks to the press outside Liverpool airport.*

*Joe Fagan addresses the crowd, appealing for calm.*

'The match paled into insignificance after the trouble I had witnessed and I just wanted to turn the clock back.'

made me realise just how serious the situation had become.'

I watched the game unaware that people had died on the terraces. Surely they wouldn't play a match if people had died? The match paled into insignificance after the trouble I had witnessed and I just wanted to turn the clock back. That Liverpool lost the match 1-0 seems irrelevant when for the family and friends of the innocent victims it was a heartbreaking tragedy.

It was also a woeful manner in which to end Joe Fagan's illustrious Liverpool career. Joe was speechless, and after nearly 27 years of loyal service to Liverpool Football Club, the boot room stalwart was inconsolable. According to Roy Evans, 'he carried it with him for the rest of his days.' The Heysel tragedy left a stain on the reputation of Liverpool fans, but it also highlighted the deadly consequences of football hooliganism. As the sun set on Joe Fagan's career at Liverpool FC, it was heartbreaking that this was how his final moments as manager would be remembered.

*A weeping Liverpool fan sits outside the Liver building in the city centre following the Heysel disaster.*

# Chapter 11

The Seeds of Change – Kenny Dalglish

# The Seeds of Change – Kenny Dalglish

Kenny Dalglish had been asked by the Liverpool board to be Joe Fagan's successor before the horror of Heysel, and he had agreed to take the coveted crown as the first ever player/manager in the top flight of the English game. It was a bold move by the Liverpool directors, breaking the tradition of recruiting from within the boot room that had served the club so well. A subcommittee of John Smith (chairman), Peter Robinson (secretary) and two boot room 'old boys' Bob Paisley and Tom Saunders made the decision after lengthy discussions. The appointment came as a complete surprise to many – including Kenny Dalglish himself – but Bob Paisley's appointment as 'a special adviser' gave the fans confidence. Dalglish was unveiled the day after the Heysel tragedy, when Liverpool Football Club was at the lowest point in its history. As someone who had witnessed the horrors of Heysel, I thought the timing of the announcement revealed crass insensitivity by the Liverpool board, but maybe they thought they needed a spokesperson, or perhaps they just wanted to protect outgoing manager Joe Fagan from the inevitable media interrogation.

*Joe Fagan welcomes Kenny Dalglish at the press conference after his appointment as player-manager of Liverpool in 1985.*

Dalglish had a massive job ahead of him, but first had to answer questions about what had gone wrong at Heysel. He won general admiration for the way he handled the situation, deploying all the skills of an experienced politician in the first few weeks of his tenure. Joe didn't want to undermine Dalglish, so he slipped away quietly, even though he did go to a lot of home games and occasionally visited the boot room after matches if they won. A more involved role was open to Joe if he had been willing to step back into the inner sanctum of the boot room, but he believed it was the right time to move on and let others do their job unhindered.

*Kenny Dalglish decided he wasn't going to go into the boot room after games as he said he 'wasn't clever enough' in his autobiography. He had a bar built in his office to entertain family, friends, managers and coaches after home games but he would spend time in the boot room during the week. The times were changing.*

Heysel had cast a dark shadow over Liverpool Football Club and English clubs in general. UEFA banned all English teams from participating in Europe indefinitely, and Liverpool for an extra three years after that ban was lifted. Many of the organisers of that terrible night were convicted of negligence, receiving suspended sentences, including the head of the Belgium FA, the UEFA general secretary and the head of security on the night. Twenty-five Liverpool fans were

'As arguments raged at government level, Dalglish had to pick up the pieces and try to repair Liverpool's damaged reputation.'

extradited to Belgium for their part in the tragedy, and after a five-month trial fourteen were found guilty of involuntary manslaughter.

As arguments raged at government level, Dalglish had to pick up the pieces and try to repair Liverpool's damaged reputation. Being a player/manager his relationship changed overnight with the rest of the players. He was now called 'boss' rather than Kenny, and as he reveals in his autobiography, 'it felt strange walking into Anfield as boss. What made it easier was having Bob there, keeping an eye on me. That was a wise move by Liverpool's board.' Having Bob Paisley at his side seemed in some ways to be giving a nod to the boot room tradition, but with Joe Fagan drifting into the background it could be argued that it was simply a public relations exercise. Kenny Dalglish was his own man and had his own ideas. 'Seeing as they were good enough to offer me the job,' he reasoned, 'it was only right to say that I'd give it a go.' According to Bruce Grobbelaar, who threatened to quit after Heysel until being talked around by Dalglish, 'Kenny just took it in his stride and for the first time in a long while we actually heard Kenny Dalglish speak.'

Tensions did surface, though, and Dalglish later revealed in his autobiography that he encountered a problem with captain Phil Neal. Dalglish thought Neal was upset that the decision makers had chosen him as manager, rather than their team captain, who had been told off the record that he was being lined up for the post. 'Phil was clearly angry. He made a point of calling me "Kenny". Sometimes in training the other players would say "Kenny, er, I mean boss," which is fair enough; that's a slip of the tongue. Phil was different. His reaction was obviously calculated.' Dalglish pulled him up about it but there was no love lost between the two, especially after Dalglish took the captaincy off Phil Neal and gave it to Alan Hansen. Neal was soon on his way, but Dalglish maintains that he was acting in the best interests of the club as Steve Nicol was starting to do well at right-back.

Dalglish still had the backing of what remained of the boot room and he acknowledged it: 'There was so much knowledge, help and support. Tom Saunders was there. Ronnie and Roy stayed, and old Bob came in to help me.' Dalglish was desperate to succeed and that meant making his own decisions. By October 1985 Jim Beglin had replaced Alan Kennedy at left-back, and Steve Nicol had replaced Phil Neal. Craig Johnston and Jan Mølby became midfield regulars, and Dalglish's first signing, Steve McMahon from Aston Villa, also reinforced that area of the field. Dalglish changed a few minor things when it came to training, but the staff team would still play the 'kids' after the first team had finished or were off. If fans had been worried about a player/manager in charge, their doubts were shown to be unfounded. After a slow start and a mid-season slump – which I remember raised a few eyebrows – Liverpool went on a tremendous run, claiming 31 points from the last 11 games. In fairy-tale fashion, Dalglish scored the winning goal against Chelsea at Stamford Bridge to secure the Championship in a thrilling climax to the season, as Liverpool pipped Everton to the title.

*Liverpool celebrate after clinching their 16th League title with a 1-0 win at Chelsea.*

*Kenny Dalglish shares a joke with his new signing Steve McMahon, September 1985.*

A week later they would face their fierce rivals Everton in the first all-Merseyside FA Cup Final. In the lead-up to the clash of the best two teams in the country, Merseyside was gripped with Cup fever. This game would decide who were the 'Pride of Merseyside'. Everyone in the city seemed to be heading to London for the final and I was lucky enough to get a ticket. Everton dominated the first half and it was difficult to see how Liverpool were going to get back into the game after a Gary Lineker goal put Everton one up. Liverpool were struggling to find any rhythm as wave after wave of Everton attacks threatened more goals. We were relieved when the half-time whistle came. The second half started off in a similar fashion with Everton dominating, then out of nowhere Liverpool came back from the dead. After two goals from goal machine Ian Rush, and one from Craig Johnston, Kenny Dalglish lifted the FA Cup to join the exclusive club of managers who had achieved the double. It was a remarkable achievement in his first season. For more than two decades Liverpool had dominated English football, from Shankly to Paisley to Fagan, and now it was continuing with Dalglish – the first person outside the inner sanctum to be appointed. Even though the board had broken with the boot room continuity, it looked like their decision had been totally justified.

Top left *Howard Kendall and Kenny Dalglish lead out their teams before the first all-Merseyside Cup Final, 10 May 1986.*

Top right *Ian Rush celebrates scoring his 56th-minute goal*

Bottom left *Roy Evans chats with Howard Kendall after Liverpool's victory*

Bottom right *Liverpool (and some Everton) fans welcome the double winners*

But things were changing back at Anfield, which would have a profound effect on the future of Liverpool Football Club. In *Secret Diary of a Liverpool Scout*, Simon Hughes maintains that Everton's resurgence under Howard Kendall had a huge consequence for Geoff Twentyman's position at Anfield. His judgement had been questioned before, most notably when a director had said to him, 'That's a lot of money you've spent on a dud' – referring to Ian Rush, who had failed to find the net in his first season at Liverpool, even though he had only featured in nine games. That time Twentyman had the last laugh, as

Ian Rush went on to become Liverpool's all-time leading goalscorer with an incredible 346 goals in his Anfield career. But now the Liverpool board weren't happy that Everton had signed Gary Lineker after Twentyman had passed on him. Twentyman detected a change in attitude from the power brokers at Anfield when chairman John Smith started to grill him, and then asked for written scouting reports from the weekend on his desk by Monday morning. The writing was on the wall, and Geoff Twentyman would soon be on his way. Chris Lawler – who oversaw the reserves – would also be told he was surplus to requirements. In many ways this was a watershed moment in the history of the boot room, from which nobody had ever been sacked before. An institution based upon honesty, loyalty, trust and a collective spirit, the boot room had kept Liverpool at the top since the early 1960s, but it was about to be compromised.

Responding to criticism at the time, Kenny Dalglish wrote in his autobiography: 'One accusation levelled at me was that I dismantled the great Boot Room. That's utter rubbish. How could I damage something that was so fundamental to the success of Liverpool Football Club, past, present and future?' He also denied that the claims that he had tried to reduce the boot room's influence, saying that critics ignored the fact 'that I went in there every day of the week to talk to Ronnie, Roy and Tom. But I never went in after games for one good reason – I wasn't clever enough.' Dalglish claims the boot room thrived under him, but the unexpected sacking of Chris Lawler and the encouragement given to Twentyman to leave on medical grounds indicated that Dalglish wanted his own people in. Dalglish thought Lawler was too quiet and felt he needed someone 'with more charisma' to bring on the youngsters. Twentyman did have arthritis in his back, but it didn't stop him doing his job as he still had his eyes and ears. Dalglish insisted that 'it was right for Geoff Twentyman to leave' and that he wouldn't have done it without consultation. This points to it being a board decision, and in retrospect it seems to mark the beginning of the end for the boot room philosophy that had brought success for a quarter of a century. Maybe Dalglish wanted to stamp his authority on the set-up and wanted fresh blood, or maybe the board thought they were 'modernising' and Twentyman was 'old school'. Whatever the reason, the continuity had been broken.

Dalglish's old team-mate Phil Thompson was put in charge of the reserves and Ron Yeats was put in charge of scouting, though he had no prior scouting experience. Twentyman had given nearly 20

*Liverpool's youth squad with their coaches Chris Lawler* (back row, right) *and John 'square ball' Bennison* (far right) *in March 1986. Chris Lawler would soon be sacked from the boot room.*

years' service to the cause, keeping Liverpool at the top of domestic and European football by scouting players like Clemence, Heighway, Keegan, Neal, Hansen, Lawrenson, Gillespie, Nicol and Rush from Scottish football and the lower leagues. Sadly, in his last days at Anfield and Melwood he felt the chill wind Shankly had experienced. Geoff Twentyman's son William told me, 'As a family we were disappointed at how it all ended at Liverpool.' Roy Evans doesn't think there has ever been a better chief scout than Geoff Twentyman, who many saw as a vital cog in the boot room dynasty. Graeme Souness – who became player/manager of Glasgow Rangers in 1986 – agreed, and couldn't believe Liverpool had let the 56-year-old Twentyman leave. He quickly offered him a position as his chief scout in England. Souness believed he was getting the best scout in Britain. 'Geoff was the kind of guy that epitomised the boot room spirit and he was definitely the kind of person I wanted at my club,' said Souness.

Liverpool's loss was Rangers' gain, as he went on scouting for them until his retirement in 1991.

Kenny Dalglish was named manager of the year in 1986 – and deservedly so – but the team he had inherited was viewed as Joe Fagan's. It wouldn't be long before Dalglish would start to make the changes needed to stay at the top. The 1986/87 season was a disappointment after the success of his first one, and again the title changed hands on Merseyside, with Everton finishing nine points ahead of second placed Liverpool. In the FA Cup Liverpool had crashed out to Luton Town on their synthetic pitch, and although they had reached the final of the Littlewoods Cup they lost to Arsenal 2-1. Dalglish knew he had to act, and with the loss of Ian Rush to Juventus for £3.2 million, and a series of injuries to Jim Beglin, Kevin MacDonald and John Wark, fresh faces were desperately required. In January 1987 Dalglish bought John Aldridge from Oxford United as a replacement for Ian Rush, followed by John Barnes from Watford and Peter Beardsley from Newcastle in the summer. Ironically, it was Geoff Twentyman who had recommended, shortly before he left Anfield, that Liverpool should buy both Barnes and Beardsley as they were Liverpool-type players. With these additions to the squad, Liverpool were installed as firm favourites to win the League in 1987/88, and they didn't disappoint, finishing nine points ahead of Manchester United. Some of the football played that season was breathtaking.

The Barnes, Beardsley, Aldridge combination was unstoppable, scoring 56 goals between them. Nobody could now argue this was a team Dalglish had inherited, and it was a team overflowing with skill and creativity, just like their manager. In one game against Nottingham Forest at Anfield, Liverpool totally outclassed Brian Clough's title challengers with a brilliant display of total football. The legendary Tom Finney – a great friend and old team-mate of Bill Shankly – described the performance as 'the finest exhibition I've seen the whole time I've played and watched the game. You couldn't see it bettered anywhere – not even in Brazil.' It was one of those nights where everything came off, and as a spectator I have never witnessed anything like it before or since.

*Boot room boys in the dugout, December 1986. Ronnie Moran was quoted as saying the boot room hardly changed under Dalglish.*

*Kenny Dalglish with new signings John Barnes and Peter Beardsley at Melwood, July 1987.*

At last Dalglish had a side he could call his own, a team with individual flair and ability. The bold decisions made by the board earlier seemed to be working. Liverpool were one game away from a second double in three years under Kenny Dalglish, with only Wimbledon in the FA Cup Final standing in their way. However, the unfashionable underdogs caused one of the biggest upsets in Cup Final history by hustling and bustling the creative Liverpool side out of their stride. Wimbledon won with a headed goal from Lawrie Sanchez – for Liverpool it was a disappointing end to a thrilling season.

The 1988/89 season will be remembered for one thing – the Hillsborough tragedy on 15 April 1989, where 96 men, women and children lost their lives watching the team they loved. The fixture was a repeat of the previous year's FA Cup semi-final against Nottingham Forest, also played at Sheffield Wednesday's Hillsborough stadium, which had been relatively incident free, apart from overcrowding in the Leppings Lane end, which many fans complained to the authorities about. Their warnings fell on deaf ears and a fatal crush occurred

*John Barnes has the Forest
defence chasing shadows during
the 5-0 victory.*

in the Leppings Lane end the following year. After a systematic
establishment cover-up and smear campaign, it would take 26 years
of campaigning and heartache before the longest inquest in British
legal history returned the verdict of the jury. In April 2016 they ruled
that the 96 people had been unlawfully killed and a catalogue of
failings by the police and the ambulance services contributed to
their deaths. The Liverpool fans had been congratulated by the Lord
Justice Taylor report, commissioned by the Thatcher government
shortly after the disaster, for their 'magnificent response in initiating
a rescue operation', but a false narrative created in many sections of
the media led to one of the biggest miscarriages of justice in British
history.

I witnessed the events unfolding in the North Stand of the ground,
and after being involved in a crush outside the totally inadequate
Leppings Lane turnstiles, I took my seat just as Peter Beardsley hit
the bar in the fifth minute of the match. Within a minute a policeman
had run onto the pitch to tell the players to leave. It would turn out to

*Kenny Dalglish at Hillsborough.*

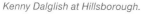

be Britain's worst ever sporting disaster. I wandered around the pitch in a state of confusion, but soon realised that the fans being carried on improvised stretchers made from advertising hoardings by their fellow fans were either dead or dying. I witnessed heroic, desperate attempts to revive victims on the field. The field of dreams became the killing fields. Kenny Dalglish and Brian Clough both came onto the pitch, but nobody had any information to give them – certainly not the line of police who I approached and asked why they couldn't help. With a shrug of the shoulders one of them answered, 'We can't do anything as we're waiting for orders.' Those orders obviously never came as they spent the best part of an hour and a half in a line across the pitch, broken only by the gaps caused by the Liverpool fans conducting the rescue operation, through their thin blue line.

When the full enormity of the disaster was known, the city of Liverpool was in deep mourning. I was completely numb and found it hard to come to terms with what I had witnessed. On the Monday

*Police officers link hands on the pitch waiting for orders that never came as the fans conducted the rescue operation.*

after the disaster, I, like many others, went to Anfield to seek some solace. I took with me my poster of Bill Shankly on the steps of St George's Hall with his arms outstretched. On the poster was his quote 'Some people believe football is a matter of life or death. I am very disappointed with that attitude. I can assure you it's much, much more important than that.' I cut the quote off the bottom, discarded it, and placed the poster on the Shankly Gates on the Anfield Road.

THE FOOTBALL ASSOCIATION
CHALLENGE CUP SEMI-FINAL

LIVERPOOL
V
NOTTINGHAM FOREST

AT HILLSBOROUGH STADIUM
SATURDAY 15th APRIL 1989 - KICK OFF 3.00 PM

NORTH STAND

GANGWAY R ROW: 43

SEAT: 158

£ 14.00
THIS PORTION TO BE RETAINED

*Above right The pitch at Anfield, covered with thousands of bunches of flowers laid as a mark of respect to the many Liverpool fans that lost their lives at Hillsborough only a few days before.*

On 30 April Liverpool took to the field against Celtic in Glasgow in a fundraising friendly in which Dalglish played. It was an emotionally charged day and I will never forget the heartfelt welcome we received from the people of Glasgow. There was no segregation, and the rendition of 'You'll Never Walk Alone' was one of the most poignant I've ever heard. I never went to the rearranged semi-final at Old Trafford or the final at Wembley, as I thought the games should never have been played, but before the semi-final the club had canvassed the victims' families who thought it should go ahead. Liverpool won the replay against Forest 3-1 to set up another all-Merseyside final on 20 May 1989. Liverpool won the game 3-2. As far as I was concerned the results hardly mattered, but if it brought some comfort to the families of the victims then it was worthwhile. Liverpool dedicated the victory to the memory of those who died at Hillsborough.

On Friday, 26 May Liverpool faced Arsenal at Anfield to decide the League title. I was still in two minds over whether football for Liverpool Football Club should have carried on that season at all, but as I was a Kop season ticket holder I decided to go. It was a sensational finale to a traumatic period in the club's history. Arsenal needed to win by two goals to snatch the title from Liverpool, as Liverpool had a superior goal difference. Deep into injury time, with Liverpool 1-0 down and the Kop whistling for the final whistle, Arsenal launched one last desperate attack. Michael Thomas latched on to a through ball and slotted it past Grobbelaar. Liverpool's dream of a double in memory of the Hillsborough victims was over. Arsenal had won the title with the last kick of the match. Despite being hugely disappointed, we gave the Arsenal team a tremendous ovation at the end – losing in a football match had to be put into perspective after the anguish of the previous weeks.

*Below Arsenal's Michael Thomas scores his side's second goal in injury time at the end of the dramatic Championship-clinching victory at Anfield, 26 May 1989.*

*Right Arsenal's Tony Adams gives an emotional John Barnes a pat on the back after Arsenal had snatched the title from Liverpool.*

In September 1989, the top scorer for the past two seasons John Aldridge was on his way to Real Sociedad, as Ian Rush had returned to Liverpool from Juventus. It could be that Dalglish just preferred the Rush/Beardsley combination up front, and his confidence in that partnership paid dividends as Liverpool lifted another title in the 1989/90 season. It would be their 18th title. After a hesitant start to the season, Liverpool famously demolished Crystal Palace at Anfield 9-0 and went on to win the League by nine points from runners-up Aston Villa. The star of the season was undoubtedly John Barnes, who won the footballer of the year award – he was quite simply sensational.

The boot room was certainly still operational, with the loyal stalwarts Ronnie Moran and Roy Evans working alongside new

*Liverpool players salute the fans after winning the 1990 League Championship.*

recruits Steve Heighway (youth development) and Ron Yeats (chief scout), but it was becoming less and less influential as the years went by. The game was modernising and so was Liverpool Football Club – the boot room was viewed by some as a relic of the past, and sawdust, beer crates, cloth caps and Guinness Export were being replaced by champagne, corporate hospitality and commercialism. Dalglish had produced one of the greatest teams Liverpool supporters had ever seen, but the deaths of 96 fans would change football forever. We didn't realise it at the time, but soon football would become unrecognisable from the glory years when the boot room ruled the world – the seeds of change had been sown.

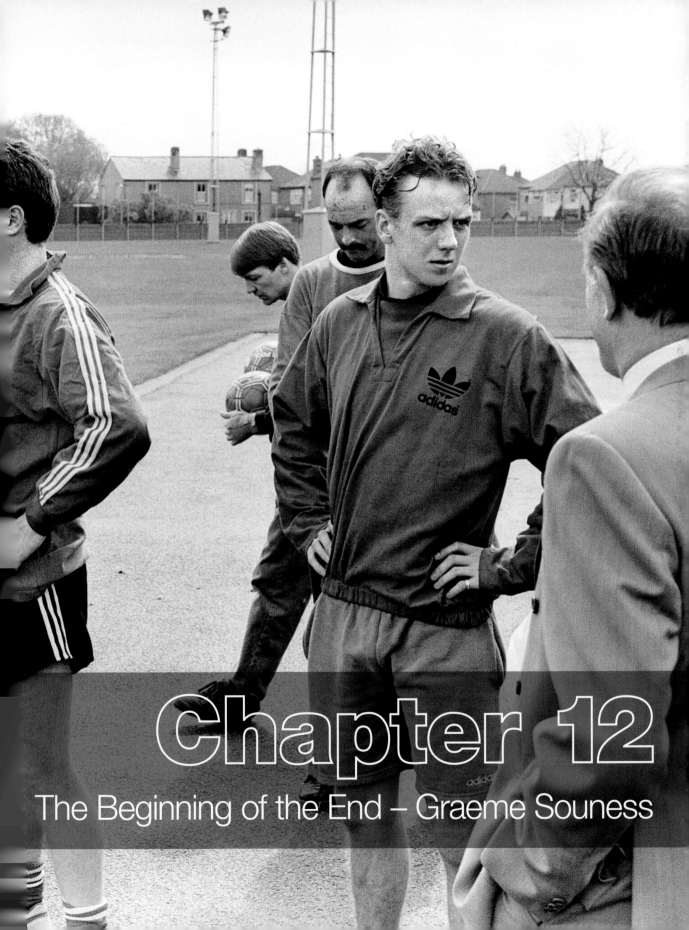

# Chapter 12

The Beginning of the End – Graeme Souness

*Action from the fifth round replay at Goodison Park which ended in a 4-4 draw after extra time. It would be Kenny Dalglish's last game in charge – he handed in his resignation a day later on 21 February 1991.*

# The Beginning of the End – Graeme Souness

Liverpool had been unconvincing in the 1990/91 season, but by the time they beat Everton in the League in February 1991 they were three points clear of Arsenal at the top. Their next match was against Everton at Anfield in the fifth round of the FA Cup. It ended in a 0-0 draw so it went to a replay at Goodison three days later. In one of the greatest derby matches in living memory the game ended 4-4 after extra time. It was a pulsating match but also nerve-wracking. Players later remembered that Kenny Dalglish was unusually quiet in the dressing room afterwards. He had made his mind up – he wanted out.

The day after the match at Goodison, Dalglish went to Anfield and dropped his bombshell – telling secretary Peter Robinson and chairman Noel White that he couldn't take it any more. It had been 22 months since the Hillsborough tragedy, and as Dalglish explained in his autobiography, 'The strain kept on growing until I finally snapped.' He had made his mind up in the team hotel before the match that he was going leave whatever the score, for the sake of his 'sanity'. That day at Goodison he was the only person in the ground who knew he

*Kenny Dalglish announces his resignation at a press conference at Anfield, only a few days after his team's 4-4 draw with Everton.*

was leaving, and just like Shankly's resignation, it took everyone by surprise. He had been Liverpool's manager for five and a half years and had dealt with the aftermath of two of football's biggest disasters. There had been rumours of bust-ups with the hierarchy over his signings of Ronny Rosenthal, David Speedie and Jimmy Carter, who many thought were not up to Liverpool's standards. Even so, nobody had predicted his resignation.

Ronnie Moran was as bewildered as everyone else. 'We were due to play Luton away on the Saturday and I'm sat at home on the

Thursday night when the phone goes. It was Kenny and he was upset. He said, "I've packed in." I didn't believe him. I knew he could be a practical joker, so I replied, "Come on, what do you really want?" "No," he said, "I've packed up, I've really packed up. I've finished. I've resigned." I still couldn't believe what he was telling me, but he started getting a bit overcome with emotion and put the phone down.'

The following day Noel White announced: 'It was with great regret that we learned of his decision to resign as team manager. I would like to assure our supporters that we did everything in our power to change his mind, and to continue to do the job which he has done with such conspicuous success during the last five years or so.' Having reluctantly accepted Dalglish's resignation, the board then asked the boot room's Ronnie Moran to take over for the next few games until they decided on who would replace him. For the best part of two months, the caretaker manager took the reins, but Liverpool's form unfortunately slumped, and they lost touch with eventual winners Arsenal. Jan Mølby was confident that the players would rally around, as were the rest of the team, especially with a boot room boy at the helm, but it never happened, as he recalls. 'The first league game after Kenny resigned I think we were three or four nil down at Luton, and the writing was on the wall.'

*Caretaker manager Ronnie Moran is all smiles before his first game in charge (left). Then he feels the pressure as he sits in the dugout with Bruce Grobbelaar (left) and Roy Evans. In the background wearing a cap is Tom Saunders.*

Ronnie Moran – who was totally and utterly committed to Liverpool Football Club – was the bookies' even money favourite to become the permanent manager, with Alan Hansen, Graeme Souness, John Toshack, Phil Thompson and Phil Neal also in the running. But Ronnie wasn't really comfortable in the limelight. 'I spoke to the chairman and told him that I couldn't do the job long term,' said Moran. 'I would only have been cheating them and I told them I wanted to go back to doing what I had been doing in the background.

The situation wasn't without its humour. At one point Alan Hansen announced to Ronnie Moran, Roy Evans and Tom Saunders in the changing room at Anfield that he had been hired as manager. He left, waited outside to listen to their reaction, then reappeared to tell them it was a 'wind up'. He played the same trick on the players, saying,

*New manager Graeme Souness with Ronnie Moran at Anfield after his appointment, 16 April 1991.*

'I spoke to the chairman and told him that I couldn't do the job long term.'

'The board have offered me the job and I've taken it. Things are going to change. I know where you live and which pubs and clubs you go to. Your drinking has got out of hand and it's going to have to stop. Steve Nicol, you are not allowed to go out to the pub ever again.' Hansen went on to say that there would be training every day and Steve Nicol was the new captain. Hansen left the stunned players in the dressing room before returning a few minutes later to tell them he was only joking, and he was retiring instead.

Liverpool lost their top of the table clash with Arsenal 1-0 at Anfield, their third loss in nine days after Dalglish's resignation, and journalists were looking in the record books to see when this had last happened. Speculation in the press linked Liverpool with John Toshack, who was managing Real Sociedad, but a £1.5 million buy-out seemed to dampen the club's enthusiasm, and Liverpool announced that Ronnie Moran had been appointed manager until the end of the season. This seemed to boost team morale and Liverpool won three on the run. According to Ronnie's son Paul Moran, his dad then had a change of heart and told Peter Robinson and Noel White that he could do the job permanently if they wanted to offer him it. But they told him he was too late: they had since been in touch with Graeme Souness – the manager of Glasgow Rangers – who had accepted their offer.

It was all change at Anfield, which reflected the city as a whole. Liverpool had lost 20 per cent of its population over the previous decade due to the recession of the 1980s, but the mass exodus looking for work had slowed down considerably in the early 1990s. Liverpool as a city was more confident and the future looked a lot brighter than it had done at the beginning of the 1980s. It was a time of great changes at home and abroad. John Major had succeeded Margaret Thatcher, the poll tax was no more, the Soviet Union had ceased to exist and apartheid in South Africa had been abolished. For me personally it was also a special time. My group The Farm had a No. 1 album, and Cream – the club that would revolutionise dance music – was only months away from opening. Meanwhile, over in the boot room at Anfield a new regime was on the horizon.

*Souness certainly promised to change things.*

Graeme Souness's appointment as Liverpool's manager on 16 April 1991 was greeted with almost universal approval. His former Liverpool team-mates lined up to voice their delight at his appointment, but as a fan I wasn't so sure. I had observed what he had done at Rangers and was concerned that he would make wholesale changes to the set-up at Liverpool, including what was left of the boot room. Graeme Souness has since revealed that Peter Robinson – who was the recognised kingmaker at Anfield – had warned him about the size of the task facing him. When he arrived at Anfield, Souness claims Robinson said to him, 'You do know what you are taking on, don't you? We are not a good team and we don't have many great players. In fact we only have one – John Barnes.' That opinion was echoed by none other than boot room old boy, and now director, Tom Saunders, who kept on reminding him of the challenge that faced him.

Souness claims that it took him less than two months to realise 'the Liverpool of 1991 was a pale shadow of the club I had left in 1984.' He thought the club had lost its hunger and he had inherited an ageing team. He may well have had a point, as on the terraces we knew that the steady stream of players from the lower leagues identified by Geoff Twentyman and his scouting set-up had dried up after he left in 1986. Souness understood that Liverpool had been at the top for decades because they had always signed potential replacements for any first team player who had shown signs of coming to the end of his career. They bought when they were dominating, to ensure that the dynasty continued. As Roy Evans said, 'The club liked to buy two top players and a few hopefuls every season to keep at the top.' Those players would then spend their time in the reserves and would be taught 'the Liverpool way' by the boot room. That had been the template since Bill Shankly broke up the 1960s team, but Souness wrote that 'Kenny allowed that policy to slip.' He does go on to say that Hillsborough was a contributory factor, as Dalglish and his players

*The boot room in 1991.* Left to right: *Phil Thompson, Roy Evans, new manager Graeme Souness, Ronnie Moran, Phil Boersma and club captain Ronnie Whelan.*

had gone through such a horrendous and traumatic time that 'Kenny couldn't say goodbye to those players.'

Souness had always been associated with success and his first spell at Liverpool as a player had certainly been that. At that time, he was probably the best midfield player we had ever seen at Anfield: combative, skilful and fearless. He was optimistic at the press conference when he was unveiled as manager, saying Liverpool 'play the best club football of any club side in Britain, maybe Europe and maybe the world.' He'd captained a Liverpool that had conquered all of Europe under the guidance of the boot room, but in reality he was now taking over at a club that was in crisis.

Souness brought in as his assistant former Liverpool player Phil Boersma, who was with him at Rangers, and asked Ronnie Moran to continue as his chief coach. Everyone at the club thought the new regime would continue the tried and tested methods that had been in place since the early days of the boot room, but the manager had other ideas. After seeing Liverpool finish runners-up to Arsenal,

Souness decided that radical changes were needed at the club. Football was changing, and as a player at Sampdoria he had seen the emphasis on players' nutrition, so he introduced a new low-fat diet. The days of the team bus stopping off for fish and chips after an away match were a thing of the past. Folklore has it that when he heard the news, Ian Rush quipped, 'We won four European Cups on fish and chips!'

But football was entering a new sports science era, and Souness was intent on modernising Liverpool Football Club so as to compete in the 1990s. Maybe he tried to change too many things too quickly, because the changes were not popular with the players or the boot

*FC Kuusysi Lahti v Liverpool. Manager Graeme Souness watches the action with assistants Ronnie Moran, Roy Evans and Tom Saunders on the bench. It was Liverpool's first away game in Europe since the Heysel stadium disaster in 1985. Liverpool were a shadow of that team, losing 1-0 to the Finnish part timers, even though they had won 6-1 at Anfield in the first leg.*

room. For example, he decided that meeting up at Anfield and getting a coach to Melwood, like they had done since the Bill Shankly days, was a thing of the past. He wanted Melwood to be their headquarters, and the board of directors must have agreed, as that's exactly what happened. The press also reported that Souness had ordered the boot room to be demolished, but that actually isn't true. The Premier

League was being formed and they demanded better press facilities at every ground, so the boot room was eventually sacrificed to make way. As Peter Robinson put it, 'Football was moving on. We also needed to have an after-match press room and the boot room was the ideal area for it.'

Roy Evans thinks Souness has been blamed unfairly for the decline in form. 'The team Kenny left him wasn't the best, but he kept all the staff on,' says Evans. In actual fact, it was the hierarchy of the club that took many of the decisions. Peter Robinson certainly thought Liverpool had to move on from the Shankly period, and I know a supporter who had a massive row with then chairman David Moores, who had suggested that he was sick of hearing about Bill Shankly and the boot room and they had to make their own history. Souness was active in the transfer market, and in the summer of 1991 he bought defender Mark Wright and forwards Dean Saunders and Mark Walters, who had done well for Souness at Rangers. But he also controversially transfer-listed Peter Beardsley, Steve McMahon, Ray Houghton and Steve Staunton. In his autobiography, Souness admits with hindsight that he should have tried to keep the senior pros as he looked for replacements, but he implies they had their own priorities, as 'they were approaching the veteran stage and were looking for another move.'

John Barnes reveals in his autobiography that he never got on with Souness, as they disagreed on many issues including the way Liverpool played. He got the impression Souness didn't rate him, but they never had a full-blown argument. He felt 'everything Souness did was for the good of the club,' but goes on to say 'he got rid of too many players too soon,' and that 'all these drastic changes ran counter to Anfield's tradition of continuity, of bringing players in and phasing others out. Souness obviously felt radical steps were required and wanted his own men in.'

Roy Evans says he did get on with 'Charlie' – which was the nickname they had for Souness – and maintains 'he was the most passionate of all the managers, apart from maybe Shanks, and he was desperate to do well.' Evans thinks that where Souness went wrong

*Graeme Souness, still recuperating after undergoing major heart surgery in April, talks to Steve Nicol during a visit to Melwood in May ahead of the 1992 FA Cup Final against Sunderland.*

in the transfer market was that he tended to buy players who were physical rather than technically gifted.

The new training regime also resulted in the treatment room being at full capacity. Ian Rush blamed the spate of pulls and strains on the new schedule brought in by Souness, and it was clear the players and coaches weren't happy with the changes. Liverpool's form was dire at the beginning of the 1991/92 season due to all the injuries and departures, and by the end of October they were eighth in the table. Even after trying to strengthen the team mid-season with the addition of full-back Rob Jones from Crewe, midfielder Michael Thomas from Arsenal and István Kozma, the Hungarian international midfielder, from Dunfermline, the team struggled to find any form and finished sixth. It was their worst position for 27 years. There were some positives as Steve Heighway's youth system began to bear fruit – and promising youngsters like Steve McManaman and Mike Marsh emerged – but there was no doubt Liverpool were declining rapidly.

During the season, a medical check-up revealed that the 38-year-old Souness had heart disease, and soon after Liverpool's FA Cup semi-final victory against Portsmouth it was announced that he needed emergency triple bypass surgery. During his period of recuperation Souness did something which many fans still find it

*Jan Mølby* (above left) *and Steve McManaman* (above) *in action in the 1992 Cup Final against Sunderland, which Liverpool won 2-0. Above right Ronnie Moran celebrates with Graeme Souness.*

difficult to comprehend. He sold an exclusive to the *Sun* newspaper, even though it had been boycotted on Merseyside because of the false allegations it published soon after the Hillsborough disaster. They ran the Souness piece on 15 April 1992 on the third anniversary of the disaster. Souness later made a full apology and donated the fee to Alder Hey Children's Hospital, but the damage was done. Souness defended himself by saying that he was manager of Rangers when the Hillsborough disaster occurred, and the Scottish version of the paper bore little resemblance to the English version. He claimed he wasn't aware of the depth of feeling against the paper and it was a genuine mistake, but later he conceded that 'it just went from bad to worse for me after that. It might have been a good idea to resign there and then.'

Winning the FA Cup that year could not disguise the fact that Liverpool was a club in turmoil, in need of surgery itself. Soon after the FA Cup Final, Graeme Souness decided to sack reserve team boss Phil Thompson. He had heard on the grapevine that while he was in hospital recovering from his heart surgery Thompson had gone into the boot room after a match against Manchester United and criticised everything Souness had done as manager. He claims Phil Thompson even did this in front of Brian Kidd, Manchester United's assistant manager, who was a guest in the boot room. 'He blamed

*Steve McManaman and his team-mates tour Liverpool after winning the FA Cup, 11 May 1992.*

me for everything,' says Souness. 'He slammed my policy in the transfer market, he ridiculed my buys and blasted me for allowing certain players to leave.' To be fair to Thompson, he had his ear to the ground and he was only expressing the supporters' opinions at the time – especially after the *Sun* exclusive – but to do it in the boot room indicated that the policy of discretion and 'omertà' was a thing of the past. The boot room boys of yesteryear would never have contemplated such an attack on their manager. Even the boot room had become dysfunctional.

Football itself was entering a new era. A global brand was about to emerge that would transform English football, with clubs becoming investment vehicles for people with little interest in the actual game. The Premier League was light years away from the boot room and their philosophies, principles and love of the game. It was the Hillsborough disaster that changed everything and paved the way for a money-spinning industry fed by staggering worldwide television revenues. The first interim report by Lord Justice Taylor identified the particular causes of the Hillsborough disaster, but the second final report, which focused on safety generally, was damning about the governance of football and the condition of football stadiums. Clubs then accepted Taylor's 'recommendation' for all-seater stadiums without the agreement of supporter organisations.

In David Conn's *The Football Business*, it is claimed that at a meeting over dinner in 1990, representatives of the 'self-elected' big five clubs, Liverpool's Noel White and Peter Robinson, Everton's Philip Carter, Manchester United's Martin Edwards, Arsenal's David Dein and Tottenham Hotspur representative Irving Scholar, had discussed the idea of a breakaway league with London Weekend Television executive Greg Dyke. The deal for the TV rights Greg had secured for ITV in 1988 was due to run out in 1992. The big five were unhappy at sharing the growing TV revenues with other, smaller clubs, wanting more of the money for themselves. After the meeting, Noel White and David Dein went to see the FA to see if they would back their breakaway from the Football League. In David Conn's words, 'The FA to its shame, betraying its historic role as regulator, controller of commercialism for the wider good of football, was to put its name to the breakaway which would make a fortune for the owners of the big clubs and open up enormous inequality in football.' Ironically, Greg Dyke eventually lost out to Rupert Murdoch's Sky TV in the bidding war that would transform the domestic game beyond all recognition.

Liverpool may have been one of the big five who were instrumental in the formation of the Premier League in 1992, but their fortunes on the pitch were spiralling downwards. It even prompted club chairman David Moores to deliver a message to disgruntled supporters: 'Being half-way down the Premier League and out of the three major Cup competitions is totally unacceptable. The board have chosen to stay calm, to support the manager and team and do everything we can to overcome the present difficulties.' The board decided to turn to the boot room to try and restore their fortunes and promoted Roy Evans to become the assistant manager. As a valued member of the boot room, Evans was viewed as someone who could possibly steady the ship and provide a calming influence. It was significant that the board looked to tradition after the turmoil of the previous year. As a fan I personally thought Souness should have gone after the *Sun* interview, but this arrangement with Evans seemed to epitomise the indecisiveness and lack of leadership the club was suffering from. Under chairman David Moores Liverpool Football Club was a rudderless ship.

In an effort to reverse Liverpool's decline Souness once again went into the transfer market, signing Nigel Clough from Nottingham Forest for £2.2 million, Neil Ruddock from Spurs for £2.5 million and Julian Dicks in exchange for talented youngsters David Burrows and Mike Marsh. The treatment room was still bursting at the seams, and a few months into the 1993/94 season it was reported that over 20 first team players were injured. The new training system was obviously

*Goalmouth action in a Premiership match against Newcastle at St James's Park, a 3-0 defeat for Liverpool.*

not working, and Glenn Hysén was among the players who couldn't understand why Souness had changed a tried and trusted routine. 'He knew how things were done at Liverpool and won endless titles doing it the boot room way. He knew first hand it worked. Therefore, changing it didn't make sense.' The transfer policy was confusing as well. Geoff Twentyman had always been told to recruit players with a 'northern soul', but the likes of Ruddock and Dicks were anything but.

'The third-round exit to Bristol City, who won 1-0 at Anfield, was the final straw, and a few days later it was all over for Souness.'

Time was running out for Souness as their League form was still inconsistent. By the time they drew with Wimbledon 1-1 at Anfield at the end of December 1993 – their fourth consecutive draw in the League – they were languishing in eighth place, 20 points behind leaders Manchester United. There was one last glimmer of hope for silverware with the FA Cup. On 8 January 1994 Liverpool played Bristol City in the third round at Ashton Gate, but during the match the floodlights failed and the referee abandoned the match. Eleven days later, a 1-1 draw meant a replay at Anfield, but the lights were also about to go out on Graeme Souness's managerial career. The third-round exit to Bristol City, who won 1-0 at Anfield, was the final straw, and a few days later it was all over for Souness.

The appointment of Souness, which had been an attempt to move away from the boot room philosophy and its tried and trusted

methods that had kept Liverpool successful since the days of Shankly, had ultimately ended in failure. He had given youngsters like Steve McManaman and Robbie Fowler their chance, but he had also changed too much too soon. John Barnes remembers, 'Some of the players were sorry to see him go. The rest weren't.'

When Roy Evans joined the coaching staff in 1974 John Smith had famously said, 'We have not made an appointment for today but for the future. Roy Evans will be our manager.' Twenty years later, Evans was appointed manager of Liverpool Football Club. The club had returned to the certainties of the boot room. The sun was setting on one tempestuous managerial career at Anfield, but for Roy Evans it was the dawning of a new age.

# Chapter 13

## The Resurrection – Roy Evans

# The Resurrection –
# Roy Evans

Nobody was surprised when Roy Evans was named as the successor to Graeme Souness. For supporters it was a return to the days of the boot room, and it was exactly the stability the board wanted after the turmoil of the previous years. They trusted in the wisdom of the boot room 'veterans' and Evans had no hesitation in accepting the job. Even though he was only 45 years old, he was steeped in the club's traditions, had served his apprenticeship as a player and had subsequently undertaken numerous roles over the years, from reserve team coach to assistant manager.

Roy Evans had 20 years' experience in the boot room and had been a trusted, loyal servant to the club. He says he never really had any ambition to be the manager, as that would have meant him looking for someone else's job, but that now was the time 'to implement everything I had learnt from Joe, Bill and Bob'. Senior players like John Barnes, Mark Wright and Ian Rush were delighted to see Roy Evans take over as manager, even though Barnes questioned whether Evans would be ruthless enough to turn things around as he was such

*New boss Roy Evans was steeped in Liverpool tradition, having had many successful years as the reserve team manager. Highlights included winning the Central League Trophy in 1982.*

*Roy Evans takes his first training session as the new boss, 2 February 1994.*

a lovely guy. It was almost like the popular head of PE had become the headmaster overnight. 'On the first day of training after he took over,' Jan Mølby recalls, 'the old coaching manuals from Shankly's time were out … Roy and Ronnie went through all the training sessions that had been practised and we followed the same process.' Roy Evans was returning to the methods handed down from the days when Shankly totally changed the fortunes of the club. Evans was hoping for a similar transformation.

Unfortunately, results didn't improve in the 1993/94 season and Liverpool finished in eighth place, 31 points behind champions Manchester United. The last home game of the season was dubbed the Kop's Last Stand. It was to be the last home game in front of the standing Kop, which was due to be demolished that summer to make way for an all-seater stadium as recommended by the Taylor Report in the wake of the Hillsborough disaster. On an emotional day, with legends like Albert Stubbins, Billy Liddell, Tommy Smith and Kenny Dalglish paraded in front of an adoring Kop prior to the match, Liverpool lost 1-0 to Norwich. The Jeremy Goss goal in the 35th minute would be the last goal scored in front of the famous old terrace. The symbolism wasn't lost on those of us watching from our beloved Kop.

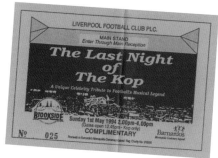

*My memorabilia from the 'Last Night of The Kop' – The Farm were privileged to perform in front of the famous terrace the day after the last game of the season against Norwich. The mighty Kop was demolished that summer.*

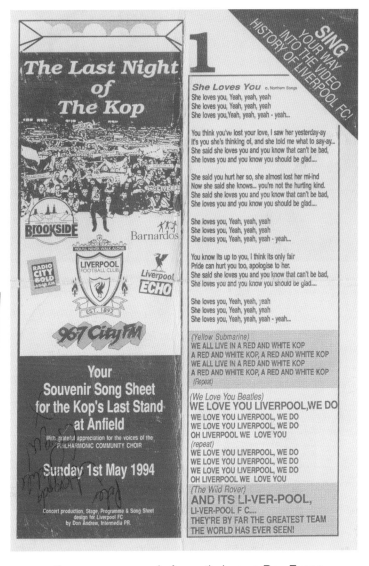

In the summer, there were grounds for optimism as Roy Evans restructured his backroom staff. He recruited sought-after coach Doug Livermore, who had played in the reserves with him during the Shankly era, and sold defenders Julian Dicks and Torben Piechnik. He recruited centre-backs Phil Babb from Coventry, who had impressed for Eire in the 1994 World Cup, and John Scales from Wimbledon. Liverpool started off like the old days and after three games they were top of the League having won all three. Liverpool had annihilated Arsenal at Anfield, with a young Robbie Fowler scoring a record-

breaking hat-trick in just 4 minutes, 33 seconds. Supporters started to believe the nightmare was over and the return to boot room methods had restored Liverpool's fortunes.

Sadly, it didn't last, as their form wasn't consistent enough to stay at the top. Half-way through the season they were in third place, seven points behind leaders Blackburn Rovers – playing under manager Kenny Dalglish, who had joined them after he left Liverpool – and six behind Manchester United. Nevertheless, the promising blend of senior players and youth did bring Roy Evans a trophy in his first full season. In April 1995 they won the League Cup (then known as the Coca-Cola Cup), and although this would have been routine in the glory days of Bob Paisley and Joe Fagan, it was a welcome relief to Liverpool fans as it augured well for the future. It was Liverpool's first trophy in three years and a break from all the doom and gloom that had preceded it. Steve McManaman was unstoppable on the day and scored the two goals to see off Bolton Wanderers. The boot room appeared to have reversed the decline, and once again players were playing with a smile on their faces. On the last day of the season Kenny Dalglish brought Blackburn Rovers to Anfield, and even though they lost 2-1 to Liverpool they were crowned champions, one point above Manchester United who were only able to draw 1-1 with West Ham. Evans and Moran were genuinely pleased for Dalglish, but also

felt melancholic as five years earlier they had been celebrating a title victory for Liverpool.

By winning the League Cup Liverpool had qualified for the UEFA Cup, and in the close season Stan Collymore was signed from Nottingham Forest for a record £8.5 million to bolster the attack. Early in the 1995/96 season Jason McAteer was bought for £4.5 million from Bolton to strengthen the midfield and, for the first time in years, supporters were confident that the good times were just around the corner. When Collymore made his debut at Anfield against Sheffield Wednesday, I was in the Kop to see him scoring a wonder goal from 25 yards, and we all agreed that he was the missing piece of the jigsaw.

We all thought the tide had turned, and with Fowler and McManaman alongside Collymore the possibilities seemed endless. The free-flowing football Liverpool played that season was reminiscent of old times, and it had the TV pundits purring. Enthusiasm was dampened when Liverpool made an early exit from the UEFA Cup at

*Roy Evans, named manager of the month in January 1996, flanked by Robbie Fowler (left) and Stan Collymore, who shared the player of the month award.*

the hands of Brøndby, but their domestic form improved dramatically under the guidance of Evans. That season, Liverpool were also involved in what is still regarded as the Premier League's greatest game, when they beat Kevin Keegan's exciting Newcastle team. The match was end-to-end action with the lead changing several times and a dramatic 90th minute winner by Collymore. It was a massive blow to Newcastle's title aspirations, but for Liverpool supporters it was sweet revenge for Newcastle knocking Liverpool out of the Coca-

*Despair for Newcastle United defender Steve Watson as Liverpool forward Stan Collymore celebrates his dramatic last minute winner to win the match for the Reds in front of a jubilant Anfield crowd, 3 April 1996.*

*John Barnes in full flow in what is regarded as the best ever Premier League game.*

Cola Cup a few months earlier.

Liverpool reached the FA Cup Final that year against fierce rivals Manchester United, who had just been crowned champions. Unfortunately, the final didn't live up to all the hype, and after a dull affair that looked destined for extra time, Liverpool lost 1-0 to a Cantona strike in the 86th minute. Far from being forgotten, however,

*Tony Warner, Mark Kennedy, Dominic Matteo, John Barnes and Mark Wright (right) on the pitch at Wembley before the start of the 1996 FA Cup Final against Manchester United.*

the occasion became notorious for the white Armani suits worn by the Liverpool squad. The recriminations started soon after.

Liverpool supporters were incensed that the players seemed more interested in modelling assignments and nightclubs than winning football matches. Football had changed dramatically since the formation of the Premier League in 1992, and players had more power, more wealth and many were willing to flaunt it. Magazine interviews with Liverpool players had helped transmit the image, and soon the press had dubbed Liverpool the 'Spice Boys'. For the final, I was staying in a hotel on the London's Edgware Road where it was rumoured the Liverpool team were going to have their party if they won the Cup. The party turned into a wake as we drowned our sorrows, discussing the match at length. We were told Fowler and McManaman had gone home on the train after the match, but some of the players were going to the Chinawhite nightclub in the West End, and a few of my mates, Paul Davis, Paul Murphy and Peter Edwards,

*Steve McManaman of Liverpool challenged by Denis Irwin.*

went on a mission to 'discuss' the match with them. As some of the team stepped onto the roped-off red carpet area of the celebrity hangout, one of my mates shouted, 'You never turned up today.' One the players shouted back, 'Who the fuck are you, you wanker?' To which my mate replied, 'We're the wankers who pay your fucking wages. You should be ashamed of yourselves coming to a party after that shite.' The players, seeing the accusers meant business, shuffled their way inside. I always think to myself that Shankly would have been proud of my mate's outburst, remembering the time in 1971 he told supporters at St George's Hall that the players were privileged to play for them – even if by 1996 it wasn't the supporters who were paying the lion's share of the players' wages; they had been inflated beyond all recognition by television revenues.

The press might have hyped the 'Spice Boy' image, but unfortunately for Roy Evans, the image stuck. Even though a boot room boy was in charge, it was fundamentally a clash of two conflicting worlds. The first was a world of integrity, honesty, principles and hard work, as epitomised by Evans and Moran. The other was a world of conspicuous wealth as epitomised by the new breed of Premier League footballers who were more likely to feature in fashion magazines than football publications. Rumours started to abound that discipline was a major problem, even though Liverpool were playing some of the best football we had seen since we last won the title in 1990. When the rumour mill starts in Liverpool it goes into overdrive, and thanks to the Armani suits there were plenty of people willing to spread hearsay.

The Liverpool team were certainly entertainers on the pitch, and if they had managed to follow that up with silverware then they would have silenced their critics. But the perception was that the discipline was not what it should have been. Supporters looked down the M62 enviously, believing that Alex Ferguson had instilled a winning mentality and an iron-fisted discipline into Manchester United's set-up. Captain John Barnes agreed, but other players were saying, 'If certain players are not training hard then I'm not.' Barnes thought Liverpool had the best team in the country, but he was dismayed at the attitude to training. This frustrated him so much that he said it became an obsession. He had a word with Roy Evans, who agreed.

According to Evans, Stan Collymore 'had skill, strength stamina, speed and flexibility but his attitude wasn't the best. He wouldn't move to Liverpool from Cannock, so he was turning up late and sometimes not at all. It had a negative effect on discipline in the end, so we had to move him on. Stan never fulfilled his potential.' If Liverpool had still had a boot room scout like Twentyman, they would probably never have bought Collymore as he certainly didn't possess a 'northern soul'. Ronnie Moran even had a nickname for Collymore, calling him 'Fog in the Tunnel' due to his excuses for his timekeeping as he commuted to Melwood from Staffordshire.

In the 1995/96 season Liverpool finished third on 71 points behind champions Manchester United and runners-up Newcastle. The Liverpool board backed Roy Evans in the summer of 1996, buying Patrik Berger from Borussia Dortmund, but even though they challenged for the Championship, they just fell short. They needed a win on the last game of the season against Sheffield Wednesday at Hillsborough to come second and qualify for the lucrative Champions League. In those days only the top two English teams qualified for Europe's top competition. Liverpool could only manage a draw and ended up finishing fourth. Although the supporters were remarkably patient, they were beginning to voice their feelings about the lack of winning mentality and aggression on the field.

Attention turned to Paul Ince, the ex-Manchester United 'enforcer' who was now playing in Italy with Inter Milan. Roy Evans secured his signature for £4.2 million and also bought Øyvind Leonhardsen from Wimbledon, Danny Murphy from Crewe and the classy Karl Heinz Riedle from Borussia Dortmund. The board were certainly still backing Roy Evans, but it felt like the last throw of the dice. Although the £10 million spending spree raised expectations, it didn't translate to results on the field, and Liverpool once again were the 'nearly men'. Liverpool's performances swung from sublime to dreadful and it was a trophyless season. Liverpool could certainly play some exhilarating stuff, but then defensive frailties let them down again and again. Roy

*Patrik Berger impressed for the Czech Republic at Anfield in Euro 1996 and Liverpool bought him.*

Evans maintains, 'We tried all sorts of options to solve the defensive problems; we asked about the availability of Lilian Thuram and Marcel Desailly but we couldn't attract them.' Evans was also frustrated by his efforts to buy Teddy Sheringham from Spurs and Gabriel Batistuta from Fiorentina. He claims the deals fell through as the board wouldn't back him – a claim Peter Robinson rejects – but it would appear that

*Robbie Fowler celebrates with Ian Rush after scoring a late equaliser in the derby match at Everton, 16 April 1996.*

the manager was having the same problems Shankly had all those years ago in trying to convince the board about potential signings.

By half-way through the 1997/98 season the board had decided that the return to the boot room philosophy wasn't producing the necessary results to get Liverpool back on their perch. It was even rumoured that Kenny Dalglish might return as director of football, but in the end they decided that they should look abroad to try and remedy the situation. In 1998 France had won the World Cup and Arsène Wenger – Arsenal's French manager – was transforming English football with his stylish brand of attacking play. Liverpool were falling further behind Manchester United and Arsenal, and even though they were playing some fantastic football themselves at times, the clock was ticking; it was three years since their last trophy and eight since they had last won the League. Fans still backed the manager, but the board thought they needed to act, so Robinson got in touch with Gérard Houllier, who as technical director had helped guide France to World Cup success.

Roy Evans knew the Liverpool board had approached Houllier. The board, who were already getting a reputation for indecision, now in a classic fudge asked the two men to work together. Ronnie Moran had retired (against his wishes), so Houllier brought a coach with him called Patrice Bergues. It was truly the end of the boot room philosophy and the beginning of the French revolution. The last of the boot room boys, Evans was now being put in an impossible situation behind the scenes. The doomed managerial experiment only lasted a few months before Evans decided to walk. 'They tried hard to keep me, and they tried to talk me out of leaving. I don't blame anyone else but me. The club arranged for a meeting when the joint manager title was discussed. I should've been a bit stronger in many ways – I should've said joint managers won't work. I shouldn't have agreed to it, I should've been stronger, but I was a Liverpool fan at heart and I thought I was doing the best for the club.' Houllier was saying one thing and Evans another, and something had to give. Relations became strained, and once Houllier settled in he became more and more forceful. He started to make changes to the team and the two started to disagree on squad rotation. Evans was also upset that whenever a player was to be dropped he was the one who would have to give the player the unwelcome news, even though they had agreed to do it together. Houllier never seemed to be around when the bad news was being given out and Evans started to resent it.

He felt hurt by the decisions that undermined him, but as a loyal

Robbie Fowler displays a
T-shirt in support of the
Liverpool dockers' strike.

club man he went quietly. He was offered another role, but he didn't
want to be 'a ghost on the wall'. As Roy Evans and chairman David
Moores both fought back tears at the press conference, everyone
knew the significance of the day. The Shankly lineage had been
broken once and for all. There were tears at Melwood too, when the
canteen staff and players were informed that Roy was leaving, such
was the respect they had for him. In a broken voice David Moores
confirmed that Gérard Houllier would be in sole charge, then also
announced the surprise return of Phil Thompson: 'Phil is passionate
about the club and desperately wants success. Losing Roy is not
ending the boot room tradition. We have Sammy Lee here still.' David
Moores was fooling himself – all the original members of the boot
room had gone. Phil Thompson and Sammy Lee were steeped in the
traditions of Liverpool Football Club, but the spirit of the boot room
was no more. The 'Liverpool way' was a distant memory, effectively
undermined in the Dalglish years and broken in the Souness years.

Liverpool Football Club had enjoyed three decades of
unprecedented success from the 1960s to the early 1990s, and had
dominated domestic and European football. After Bill Shankly had
delivered the impossible dream, his trusted lieutenants Bob Paisley,

An emotional Roy Evans at the press conference to announce his retirement as Liverpool's joint manager, 12 November 1998.

'The boot room was the think tank of Liverpool FC, like a university of football but devoid of pretension.'

Joe Fagan, Reuben Bennett, Ronnie Moran, Geoff Twentyman, Tom Saunders, John Bennison and Roy Evans had continued the collective endeavour for the good of the club. They were of their time, principled and dedicated, and possessed a Midas touch. The boot room was the think tank of Liverpool FC, like a university of football but devoid of pretension, and a place where people who were obsessed with the game could talk endlessly about it. Some players may have seen it as an old-fashioned place where 'old men' discussed football but it was populated by people committed to winning and turning Anfield into a 'fortress'.

The unity and solidarity of the boot room was unique, and in many ways, it was a product of the backgrounds and personalities of the inhabitants. They were humble and devoted to the cause, and they never let the players get big-headed. As soon as the team had won something, be it one trophy or a treble, the boot room boys would bring the players down to earth by pointing out that it was the next season that counted, not the previous season.

The mythology of the boot room and their collective wisdom terrified opposing managers and teams. Liverpool had a psychological advantage over teams before they even played them. Watford chairman Elton John, who visited the boot room – he famously asked for 'pink champagne' but was told by Joe Fagan they only had brown ale, a Guinness or a Scotch – said, 'I felt more nervous going into that little room than playing to 100,000 people at an American concert.' Tommy Docherty remembers, 'There's only one thing I always looked forward to from a game at Liverpool – a beer in the boot room. And that was all you got.'

The boot room was the heart of Liverpool Football Club, where players feared to tread, where visitors invited into it would be thrilled. But all things come to an end, and even though the boot room was the inner sanctum of Liverpool's unprecedented success, it was always about the wisdom of the people in it rather than the bricks and mortar. By the time Roy Evans left the club, Bill Shankly, Reuben Bennett and Bob Paisley had all passed away; Joe Fagan, Geoff Twentyman and John Bennison had all retired; and Tom Saunders had become a director. The boot room conjures up so many images, but fundamentally it was about a group of closely knit people all working together with a common goal, honourable, hardworking and honest. They were a team, a band of brothers, and their memory echoes down the ages: they are quite simply 'the Immortals'. As Bob Paisley said, 'Other people have earned more money than me in football but no one has enjoyed it as much as me.'

Thanks for the memories – the Boot Room Boys are the soul of Liverpool Football Club and will never be forgotten. Shankly may have been the catalyst, but the boot room effectively created the global club we know today and their spirit lives on!

Right *Ghosts of the boot room. Brushing away memories of the past glories. Rubble and an old pair of boots are all that remains of the famous Anfield inner sanctum, 21 January 1993.*

'The boot room was the heart of Liverpool Football Club, where players feared to tread, where visitors invited into it would be thrilled.'

# Bibliography

## Books

Jeff Anderson with Stephen Done, *Official Liverpool FC Illustrated History*, Carlton 2004

John Barnes, *The Autobiography*, Headline 1999

David Conn, *The Football Business*, Mainstream 1997

Derek Dohren, *Ghost on the Wall: The Authorised Biography of Roy Evans*, Mainstream 2004

Kenny Dalglish with Henry Winter, *Dalglish: My Autobiography*, Hodder & Stoughton 1996

Andrew Fagan and Mark Platt, *Joe Fagan: Reluctant Champion*, Aurum Press 2011

Alan Hansen, *A Matter of Opinion*, Transworld 1999

Ian Herbert, *Quiet Genius: Bob Paisley, British Football's Greatest Manager*, Bloomsbury 2017

Simon Hughes, *Secret Diary of a Liverpool Scout*, Trinity Mirror Sport Media 2009

Simon Hughes, *Men In White Suits: Liverpool FC in the 1990s*, Bantam 2015

Stephen F Kelly, *Bill Shankly: The Biography*, Virgin Books 1996

Stephen F Kelly, *The Boot Room Boys*, Collins Willow 1999

John Keith, *The Essential Shankly*, Robson Books 2001

Paul Moran, *Mr Liverpool: Ronnie Moran*, Trinity Mirror Sport Media 2017

Brian Pead, *Liverpool: A Complete Record 1892–1986*, Breedon Books Sport 1986

Mark Platt, *The Red Journey: An Oral History of Liverpool FC*, DeCoubertin Books 2017

Ivan Ponting and Steve Hale, *Liverpool in Europe*, Carlton Books 2005

Adam Powley and Robert Gillan, *Shankly's Village*, Pitch Publishing 2015

*Shankly: The Lost Diary*, Trinity Mirror Sport Media 2013

Bill Shankly with John Roberts, *Shankly: My Story*, Trinity Mirror Sport Media 2011

Graeme Souness with Mike Ellis, *Souness: The Management Years*, Andre Deutsch 1999

Ian St John, *The Saint: My Autobiography*, Hodder & Stoughton 2005

Eugene Weber, *You'll Never Talk Alone*, Bluecoat Press 2006

## Articles

David Conn in *The Guardian*
*Liverpool Echo* and *Daily Mirror*
Liverpool FC programmes 1950–1998

## Websites

www.lfchistory.net
www.LiverpoolFC.com

## Documentary

Shankly: Nature's Fire, Riverhorse 2017

# Index

Page references in *italics* indicate images.

# Acknowledgements

I would like to thank my dad for bringing me up a Liverpudlian and for taking me to the match as a youngster, which led to me falling in love with football and Liverpool Football Club in particular. To my wife Geraldine for encouraging me to write the book and all her patience as I became obsessed with old photographs from the Mirrorpix archive. I would also like to thank the whole family for putting up with the books, programmes, newspaper clippings and photographs strewn around the house for many, many months. Also, to everyone I know/have known from the match, but especially all my friends in Block 306 on the Kop. Thanks to Ste Mono, Kieth Culvin and John Nicolson: the Liverpool Echo 'Allez les Rouges' podcast regulars, who in many ways remind me of the boot room boys, dedicated and loyal to Liverpool Football Club. To all the Spirit of Shankly committee/members/supporters who keep Bill Shankly's name and memory resounding through the decades.

I received a phone call out of the blue from Lorna Russell from Virgin Books who asked me if I would be interested in writing a book about the Liverpool boot room. My initial thoughts were 'what could possibly be written about the boot room that hadn't already been covered?'. But after several visits to the Reach PLC archive in Watford with the priceless help of Simon Flavin, archivist and 'Evertonian' Vito Inglese and Lucy Oates, I knew we had uncovered many incredible unpublished photographs. I thought I knew a lot about the history of Liverpool Football Club and the boot room but I've learnt so much doing my research; it's been an absolute revelation. Hopefully we have opened a window on a unique group of men who were completely dedicated to the success of Liverpool Football Club.

I would like to thank everyone who has helped me out and encouraged me during the writing of the book especially Simon Hughes, Mark Platt, Brian Reade, David Luxton, Lucy Oates – who has been absolutely brilliant with her support and advice – and of course Lorna Russell for giving me the opportunity to write about my heroes. I would also like to thank Roy Evans for agreeing to do an exclusive invaluable interview with me (and as a fan, it was very emotional). Thanks to William Twentyman – Geoff Twentyman's son – for the many conversations we've had. He is so proud of his dad's achievements during his days at Anfield.

I hope I have done the boot room boys story justice – we will never see their likes again. They belong to the ages!

3 5 7 9 10 8 6 4

Virgin Books, an imprint of Ebury Publishing,
20 Vauxhall Bridge Road,
London SW1V 2SA

Virgin Books is part of the Penguin Random House group of companies
whose addresses can be found at global.penguinrandomhouse.com

Design by Clarkevanmeurs Design Limited

All images supplied by MGN Limited, except the following: page 19 courtesy of Liverpool Football Club
pages 21, 46, 99, 103, 112, 191, 205, 211, 237, 241 courtesy of Peter Hooton, Eric Hooton,
Frank McPartland and Mick Potter

First published by Virgin Books in 2018

www.penguin.co.uk

A CIP catalogue record for this book is available from the British Library

ISBN 9780753552278

Printed and bound in India by Replika Press Pvt. Ltd.

Penguin Random House is committed to a sustainable future for our business, our readers
and our planet. This book is made from Forest Stewardship Council® certified paper.